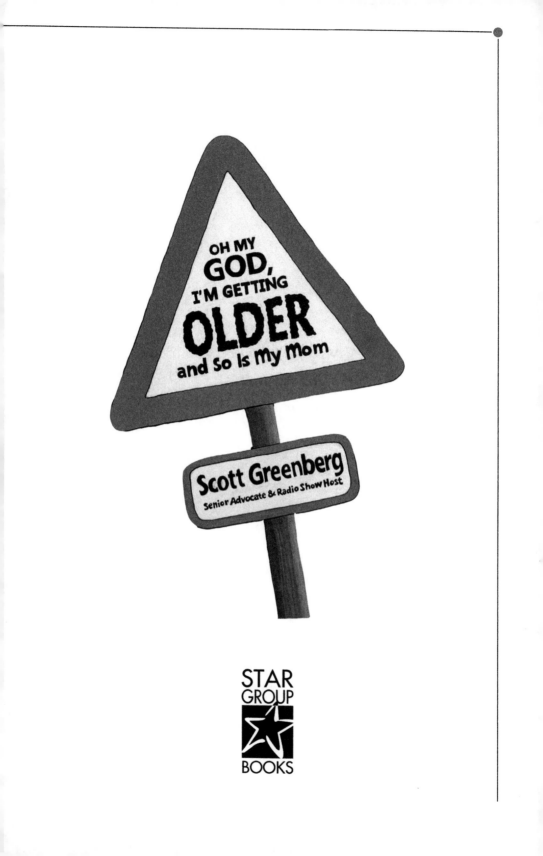

OH MY
GOD,
I'M GETTING
OLDER
and So Is My Mom

Scott Greenberg
Senior Advocate & Radio Show Host

STAR
GROUP
BOOKS

Dedication

It's always hard to single out to whom one should dedicate an effort like this. My children Melissa and Joe, and Allison and Tino, inspire me to help others prepare for perhaps taking care of their parents someday. Hopefully I've taken enough of my own advice so as not to put them in the positions I've described in the pages you are about to read.

Dedicating this to my wife Irene of 43 years seems logical. Lord knows she deserves at least that for enduring my craziness all these many decades. My grandchildren would be good choices, too, I guess, but they wouldn't appreciate the shout-out. However, I know that Irene and I would be happy to tell you that her father Leonard Weiss, who died with Alzheimer's disease, really inspires us every day to do our best to help seniors in their most vulnerable moments. So to my father-in-law Len, this book is for you.

StarGroup International, Inc. West Palm Beach, Florida

Project Coordinator: Brenda Star

Book design: Mel Abfier

Cover design: Heather Lefler

Senior Editor: Gwen Carden

Proofreader: Edie Tall

Designed and produced by StarGroup International, Inc.

(561) 547-0667

www.stargroupinternational.com

Printed in the United States of America

Library of Congress Control Number: 2013955981

Oh My God, I'm Getting Older and So Is My Mom
ISBN 978-1-884886-64-5

Special thanks to Gwen Carden and StarGroup International

Table of Contents

Foreword

If there is one thing I know for sure it is that Scott Greenberg is no ordinary man.

His deep compassion and profound perspectives of this world afford him a unique glimpse into that stage of life–old age–which we all experience if we are lucky. Scott is also a man of profound integrity who does things because they are right, not because they are easy. In this book he urges us to *take control* of our lives and make plans as carefully and with as much preparation and knowledge in this phase of life as we employed in our earlier years.

These short chapters offer deep insight, told in fable style, of how to avoid the potholes of our aging life. Through his sense of humor and inimitable style, Scott urges us to embrace our aging process by being prepared for what may come our way. I have learned much from Scott. He is a natural teacher to anyone open to hearing the lessons that have been meaningful in his life. He is a natural leader who is regularly sought out by professionals and "ordinary" folks as a resource, problem solver and trailblazer.

It is a great pleasure to write this foreword to Scott's book, as he is someone for whom I have the utmost respect and admiration. I have known Scott personally and professionally for four years and have had the privilege to present professionally with him at state and national conferences on nonprofit and business alliances and partnerships designed to offer client-centered, impactful services to older adults and their families.

I encourage you to savor these chapters and spend time digesting the imperative messages. Like kernels of popping corn, they might need to simmer awhile before taking shape.

Share this book with friends and family – anyone who might care about embracing a quality life.

> Jenni Frumer, MSEd, LMHC, LCSW, NCG
> *Associate Executive Director, Alpert Jewish*
> *Family & Children's Service*
> *West Palm Beach, Florida*

Introduction

In 2008 I was lucky enough to retire at age 58. All my dreams of carefree days at the golf course, world travel, and more time with grandchildren awaited. I had worked incredibly hard for over 20 years in the business I had just left, and I was really looking forward to every day being Sunday. Thinking I was financially secure and dreaming of the chance to do the things I always wanted to do but couldn't because of work commitments, I was fancy free and ready to enjoy the rest of my life.

And then reality hit. It was, after all, 2008 and the financial world was about to implode. Stocks tanked, real estate values crashed, interest rates began to fall and the income stream I depended on was about to be altered. Still, I had been a very conservative investor and planner and felt secure.

On Day One of my retirement, I got up, went to the gym at the club, and bumped into my friend Larry. He greeted me with the following. "I heard you retired yesterday, so when is your urologist appointment?" I laughed, but not too hard, because indeed it was scheduled for the following week. Funny? Maybe. Prophetic? Sure seemed like it. Perhaps a sign of the future? Most definitely. I spent the next 18 months living the dream. My wife Irene and I traveled with friends to Africa, spent many weeks in New York with our children and grandchildren and then took a bucket list trip to Vietnam. Of course, when the government wanted to send me there for free 40 years earlier I was less excited than I was this time around, but it was a terrific trip and much safer than it would have been in 1968. In between I played golf five times a week, exercised like crazy, read books and newspapers with great leisure, caught up on movies and watched my new reality set in. Sounds great doesn't it?

It wasn't.

I began to realize that doing nothing left a big hole in who I was. I saw my friends at the golf course, usually older than I, begin to experience things they were not prepared for. Their money was running out; their investments couldn't support them. They were getting numerous ailments, friends and family started to die off and the conversations around the bagel table turned into a Groundhog Day event of complaining about politics, their golf game, the stock market, their ungrateful kids, their annoying and needy parents, and how they missed having a purpose and things to look forward to. These were typically fairly well-to-do folks who seemingly had the world by the short hairs, yet they were miserable—and making me miserable, too.

So I did what I always do when I get bored, I got busy again. Thinking that taking care of aging retirees in

Florida might be a good business opportunity, I bought a home healthcare business. Boy was I smart, I thought. This would be a goldmine. Of course, 300 other clowns like me had the same thought, and so I entered a competitive, dog-eat-dog world I hadn't even known existed until then. You would think this world would be populated by unbelievably talented and caring people dedicated to improving the lives of seniors. Well, that was one more thing I was wrong about.

I discovered that many people who claim to be helping our seniors have agendas that tend to include separating them from their money to buy their product or service, whether it's good for them or not. I also discovered that seniors who found themselves at the mercy of this field were often completely unprepared for what lay ahead. I found people only addressing needs in crisis, enveloped in a scratchy wool blanket of confusion, family dysfunction, fear and distrust.

We are indeed living longer but not necessarily healthier, and we're running out of resources to live the dream we've all dreamt. For many, getting older is a nightmare–not just for Mom and Dad but for Baby Boomers and their kids, too.

So now after four years of my new vision and observation of the aging dynamic, I've decided to write this book. I don't want to scare people, and I don't want to sell anything except perhaps a few copies of this book. I want to show you that preparation and planning beat crisis management every day. You can, if you think through the things that are coming at you, be better able to navigate the waters ahead.

I've written some serious stuff in a lighthearted manner and hope you will read this and find some helpful hints to get you considering things you shouldn't overlook, long before you have no choices. For example, one chapter deals with funeral planning. Thinking about how you want to be buried isn't fun, but it needs to be addressed to make things easier on the survivors you will leave behind. (For me, I just want the doctors to be sure I'm dead).

I want you to take charge of important decisions ahead of time so when unscrupulous vultures descend, your family doesn't get victimized.

Don't wake up one day and say, "Oh, My God I'm getting older and so is my mom" and not know what to do. Just as hurricane preparation helps us weather the storms here in Florida where I live, this book will (hopefully) help you weather the inevitable storms of aging. Enjoy.

Chapter One

I'm OK. I Can Do It Myself

"Grandpa Scott, I can do it myself!" five-year-old Justin said as he struggled to tie his favorite little white Nike sneakers.

I tried again.

"No, I'm OK. I can do it!" he insisted.

It took all I had not to squat down and do it for him, but I didn't. I knew that his struggle was part of the growing up process, and if he wanted help, he'd say so.

After a few tries Justin gave up, and before I could stop him he bounded into the other room, laces cascading over his foot like a plate of spilled spaghetti. A few seconds later I heard a "bump" and, on my watch, my adorable grandson had tripped on his laces and fallen, his head grazing the side of the couch. Fortunately he was OK, but

I realized too late that a point had come when I should have stepped in and protected him from himself.

Working in the field that I do, it didn't take long before I made the connection between what had happened with Justin and what happens all the time in families with aging parents.

We ask them if they need help, and they say in no uncertain terms, "I can do it myself!" or "No, I'm fine." We worry a little, but in the end we decide to believe them and go about our lives blissfully ignorant. The next thing we know we get a call from the emergency room that mom or dad fell or got confused and took the wrong medication, or something else happened that easily could have been prevented.

"I'm fine" tells you no more about what's really going on than the typical "nothing" does when you ask a child what they learned in school that day.

It can mean it's no big deal (to them) that they've been eating only cereal because they can't carry heavy grocery bags anymore or that they're not bathing regularly because getting into and out of the tub or shower is just too difficult.

I can do it myself is the cry of the Greatest Generation.

See where I'm going with this?

"I can do it myself!" is the battle cry of the proud Greatest Generation who lived through the Great Depression. Unfortunately, many of them are now engaged in the "Great Deception," especially where their children are concerned.

They feel that accepting help is the end of their independence or makes them children again, when the truth is that accepting help where it's needed actually *restores* independence by giving them their quality of life back.

In many cases parents are living in the "Land of Denial."

When Justin finally let me tie his shoes after his little fall, it didn't change a thing about who he was —he just now had safer shoes to go on with his day. It's no different when you help your parents—even ones who are stubborn.

I strongly believe that you should consider helping out your parent (or parents) if you believe they need it, even when they don't want it. By framing your actions through the filter of the point of view I'm presenting here, you'll not only feel empowered to do what you have to do but also be able to explain it to your parent in a way that will make sense to them.

In many cases parents are living in the "Land of Denial," or they will "fudge" the reality of what is going on. They don't want to worry you, after all. You have your own life and your own problems. You know that conversation. It's not supposed to "work that way." Parents take care of their children, not vice versa. (By the way, this is a very Western point of view. In many Asian cultures parents expect their children to care for them in their old age, and the children grow up knowing that that's the deal).

Western folks, however, consider asking their kids for help to be tantamount to tampering with who they are.

Well, here's an indisputable argument your parent can't ignore. When they call their doctor's office to make an appointment, does the doctor answer the phone? Of course not. That's what receptionists are for. When they arrive for their appointment, does the doctor take their vitals? No, again. Why? Because the doctor needs to spend his or her time taking care of what's really important—practicing medicine—and unapologetically enlists the help of medical assistants and other office personnel to do the more mundane tasks.

Just as the quality of the doctor's practice is enhanced with help, so is the quality of life of a parent who gets the help they need. It boils down to this: The issue shouldn't be about "leave me alone and let me die my own way" but rather, what small changes can take place so that their quality of life gets better?

So, let's talk a little bit about what you're doing—or not doing—when you visit your aging parent(s).

If you're like many people, your visits are "social." Mom or Dad say they're "fine," you make a little small talk, you fuss about something pertaining to their situation, and you leave.

Reality check: If you have *any* concerns *whatsoever,* it's time to *pay attention* and look for telltale signs that all is not well. Below are common places deficits show up.

Refrigerator

• Inspect the food there. Is there too little (an indication they aren't eating regularly)?

- Is most of the food spoiled or expired?

- Does it contain nutritious food or a lot of junky, low nutrient food?

Hygiene

- How clean is their bed linen? Soiled linen could mean they don't have the energy or strength anymore to regularly change or wash the sheets.

- How clean are their clothes? If there is a large pile of dirty clothes or they are wearing clothes that obviously need to be washed, they may not be able to handle laundry anymore.

- Do you suspect they aren't bathing or washing their hair regularly? I've heard people tell me they don't shower daily because they "don't sweat."

Physical condition and outward appearances

- Are they gaining or losing a noticeable amount of weight?

- Are they not getting their hair cut?

- Has your father stopped shaving?

- Has a parent who always dressed well stopped caring about the way they look?

- Are they not cutting their fingernails or toenails regularly?

- Can you tell they're not getting to the dentist regularly?

Social activity

- Has there been a drastic change in their social habits?

- Like my mother-in-law, did they stop or significantly cut down participation in their club or senior center?

- Are they no longer playing cards with friends?

- Have they stopped or significantly reduced how often they call or e-mail you?

You can, of course, expect a few changes with age, but when there are many of them or any of them is major, this is your cue to step up.

Take action, even if they fight you tooth and nail. It's easy to throw up your hands and say, "Mom won't let me help her." But do it anyway. Her life could depend on it.

Failing to get help can result in a poor quality of life for your parent. It pushes them into isolation, bad habits, dangerous decisions and habits that can endanger themselves and others.

There are things that are easy to do that can make a big difference without threatening their independence. For example:

- Hire someone to clean the house a couple of times a month. Make sure they do laundry and change the sheets.

- Find an organization that will deliver meals. This serves two purposes: your parent will eat better, and someone will come to their home regularly.

- If no family member lives nearby, enlist a helper to take your parent out to do their errands and doctor visits. Non-medical home care agencies are everywhere. They can help with all activities of daily living. Don't be afraid to ask for a referral.

- Contact your local Area Agency on Aging, Elder Helpline or similar organization. Find out what resources are available in your community to help older people who need assistance.

What if you're lucky enough to still have both parents but know they need help, too? Don't be surprised if your father pushes back. He's been "the man of the family" for decades and is likely to think he's doing "just fine, thank you very much!"

> **Third parties can be a powerful weapon in your arsenal.**

Try to help your "stubborn" parent who wants to do it himself (or herself) understand that it may be now or in the near future too much to continue doing without help. Explain that the stress could impact their health and thus how long they can continue doing the caregiving that they feel so strongly about doing.

And finally, third parties can be a powerful weapon in your arsenal. If your parents won't listen to you, solicit the opinion of a trusted attorney, doctor or family friend. And, of course, get on the same page whenever possible with your siblings so you present a united front.

Chapter Two

"The Talk" (Not That Talk)

My wife Irene and I took one last look at each other, shrugged our shoulders in a "here-goes-nothing" sort of way, turned the key and walked in.

"Hi, Mom," Irene said, as her mother Dinah remained seated in her favorite worn-out blue fabric recliner.

"Hello, kids," my mother-in-law said with a big grin and then, with one long breath, added, "What took you so long? You're late. I thought you'd be here an hour ago."

Irene and I had just flown in from our home in South Florida for a visit with Dinah, who lived in a modest two-bedroom co-op apartment in Queens, New York. We wanted to check up on her to be sure she was doing OK, but the truth was we had another agenda. And it wasn't the first time we'd had that agenda.

Once an active person who went to the senior center three times a week and often played cards, Dinah, now widowed, was becoming isolated. Many of her friends had died or moved to Florida, and her life consisted mostly of knitting, watching TV and doing crossword puzzles. Even her visits to the senior center had decreased to less than once a week. Her 10-year-old gray Ford Taurus with 5,000 miles on it and matching dents on all four fenders sat unused and deteriorating. We joked that Mom made periodic trips to the hospital just to meet new people to talk to.

All joking aside, we had become increasingly concerned that she might fall one day and not be discovered for hours—or worse.

After exchanging some pleasantries I cleared my throat and braced myself for what I knew was coming. Despite lacking confidence in a good outcome, I began my speech.

"Mom, Irene and I are very worried about you. We don't think you should be alone anymore. We believe you need to......"

"I.....am.....not....going....to.....a......home!" she interrupted. "I am going to stay here until I die."

Ummm, now what? Here we go again.

Then came the begging (ours). And the pleading (ours). And maybe even a little bit of guilt thrown in for good measure from us but, alas, nothing worked.

Once again we were vanquished by a little old gray-haired lady in 1950s elastic pants and an oversized will to match the oversized blouse she wore.

"What are you gonna do?" I said rhetorically to Irene in exasperation as we headed back for the airport. Oh, well.

In retrospect I understand now that even though Dinah's environment didn't support her quality of life, she had no way of knowing that a different living situation would have in fact given her *more* independence, not taken it away. Framing the situation this way would have created a whole different feel to all of us. But we didn't know that then, either. There was so much we didn't know.

"I am not going to a home!"

Five years later Dinah did fall. She broke her hip while trying to step up into a bus, and while she didn't lie undiscovered in her apartment, she never recovered from it. Following surgery, she languished in the hospital for two weeks and then died from complications. I believe that our inability to convince Dinah to agree to an alternative living arrangement led indirectly to her death. While she still could have, she probably would not have fallen if she had been in an environment built specifically to support people who are aging. And frankly, I don't feel very good about that.

We were ill-equipped to talk to my mother-in-law in a way that would have helped her see things differently. I only wish I had known then what I know now.

OK, so, let's get real here.

Nobody wants to be on either end of the "old folks home" conversation any more than they want to be on either end of the "birds and the bees" conversation between parents and adolescents. But this is an essential conversation for millions of Baby Boomers these days concerned with aging parents. The sooner the better in a lot of cases.

As with my mother-in-law, most people are going to consider going to "a home" to be defeat. Mom would say, "I don't want to be one of those old people."

You have to get started sometime, so here's what you can do.

Start by evaluating how much local support your parent has. Do you or a sibling live close enough that you can take your parent to the doctor and the supermarket and check in on them regularly? If not, the stakes of letting your parent remain "independent" get higher.

When the time comes to have "the talk," get out of your own head and make the discussion about them, not you. What I mean is, don't discuss it like they need to change just so you will feel better. Don't try to make them feel guilty for not doing what you think they should do.

Instead, come armed with plenty of non-emotionally-charged ammunition. Here are a few things to consider:

• Talk to your parent about their safety and health. "Mom, I am concerned that you could fall and no one would be here to call for help." Expect denial. "Oh, I'm not going to fall." You and I know that's most likely not the case.

• Know what type of community is appropriate for your parent at his or her stage of independence so you can make some recommendations (see explanation of various options below). Visit senior living communities in your target area. Learn about costs. What sorts of activities do they have? What requirements need to be met to become a resident? Are there accommodations available? Take brochures and videos of the community to show your parent. Research the options on the internet.

• Try to get your parent interested in a community where he or she already has friends. One of Dinah's biggest fears was going someplace where she wouldn't know anyone. Many of Dinah's friends were in residential communities in Florida, and I think Dinah would have thrived had she been able to reunite with them. We could have enlisted those friends as allies but didn't think about doing that.

- Involve your siblings or even your children in helping convince your parent that making a move is in their best interest. The more people who care about your parent who are involved in the process, the more likely it is to succeed.

- Avoid scare tactics. Logic can be more convincing than hysteria.

- Be firm. Just because your parent pushes back doesn't mean you should give up. Keep at it. Be relentless if you must. I wish we hadn't given up.

Now it's time to talk about options. First of all, not all "nursing homes" are nursing homes. "Nursing home" is sort of a generic term that has a repugnant stereotypical reputation as a smelly place that houses people staring blankly out into space from their wheelchairs. To put it simply, today's options are not your grandmother's nursing home.

Let's instead refer to the variety of choices as "long-term care options."

Here is a brief description of the types.

Independent Living

Independent living is like hotel living. It is typically set up as a community for people who do not need assistance with daily activities like cooking or dressing, and while age restrictions vary by state, 75-85 is the average age. Residents frequently occupy small houses or apartments and may have access to meals, basic housekeeping, laundry services and transportation. Independent living communities cost $2,000-$4,000 per month depending on what services you need and where it's located.

Not all "nursing homes" are nursing homes.

Assisted Living

Assisted living is similar to independent living but is the next stage. Residents tend to have some level of disability and are monitored for their health and safety. Assisted living provides assistance with activities of daily living such as medication management and bathing. Assisted living can range from $3,000-$6,000 per month based on level of care and geographical location.

CCRC (Continuing Care Retirement Communities)

CCRC's are retirement communities offering several levels of care onsite: independent living, assisted living, and skilled nursing care (the conventional "nursing home" level of care). Some may offer memory care (for people with dementia). The advantage of these communities is that should needs change, the resident does not have to relocate. Should a couple reside there and each require a different level of care they are still able to remain near one another. In many cases you "buy into" these communities and thus have some equity in them, but they are typically very expensive.

Nursing Home

A nursing home is for people who are unable to care for themselves and need continual nursing care. While the majority of residents are elderly, nursing homes care for people of all ages who are ill or who have had an accident and need intensive nursing care in order to resume life in the general population. Nursing home costs average around $8,000 per month but can be less or more. Medicare provides nursing home, or more accurately, skilled nursing coverage for a maximum of 100 days, the last 80 of which have a significant co-pay. Medicaid coverage is available in most states for people who qualify.

Memory Care

Memory care-specific assisted living communities are for people with dementia. It allows them to be closely monitored while providing appropriate freedom and activities. They are often found within assisted living facilities or nursing homes or can be self-contained individual homes within a community. Typical cost ranges from $5,000-$7,000 per month.

We know that nobody wants to go into long-term care, and most people think they'll never end up there. Heck, I'd like to die on the golf course after just after having had a hole in one.

But the fact is that a large percentage of the population will, in fact, need that sort of service during their lifetime, so I strongly recommend that you be proactive. Finding the right option for a parent is no simple matter, and trying to do so in the midst of a crisis simply doesn't make sense.

Just remember. You aren't "parking your parent" until they die. You're just doing for them what they did for you. Taking care of them.

Chapter Three

Use My Doctor. He's The Best!

If you're not retired yet, you're probably fantasizing about it. Sunny days on the golf course. Lazy afternoons reading on the beach. Visits with the grandkids. Shopping at the mall during low traffic times. Champagne toasts at sunset. Sleeping in.

Problem is, there's something big missing in most lists. At least it was in mine. It involves visits to all those "ologists." You know, the ones who poke and prod you and sometimes give you bad news.

Here is a story about what happened to me on the very first day of my new retirement from my last career that brought "ologists" stampeding onto the top of my whimsical list of retirement activities.

I was 58 years old and asking myself "What the hell do I do now?" Well, why not use my newfound extra time to get into better shape? It was the first morning that I didn't have to pay attention to the alarm clock, but I awoke early (anyway) and went to the fitness center at my golf club. A good friend of mine greeted me with: "Hey, Scott, I heard you retired yesterday. So when is your urologist appointment?"

We laughed, but I really didn't laugh that much. I actually *did* have an appointment the following week to see my urologist. Had I turned into a geezer stereotype in less than 24 hours?

It dawned on me that as we age we get introduced to one ologist after the other. There are urologists for that very special part of our anatomy, dermatologists for our skin conditions and ophthalmologists for our declining eye sight ... well, you get the picture. I don't know about you, but I'm meeting more people with big titles after their name and multiple diplomas on their wall than I ever wanted to.

> **"So when is your urologist appointment?"**

Now I visit my gastroenterologist for a regularly scheduled meeting. Of course the meeting I'm talking about is a pair of rubber tubes going in from both ends until they meet in the middle. At that point, the meeting is over.

From there I go to the cardiologist to make sure the ticker is going to keep on ticking. How about the hematologist for my blood work? Can't forget that, can we? And then what if, God forbid, we have a scare?

Now we sit on pins and needles waiting for the **path*ologist's*** report. If it's bad news, we get introduced to onc**ologists** and then to psych**ologists** to manage our emotions so we can begin to deal with what lies ahead.

Oy vey, what happened to my dreams of moonlit nights on the beach with a glass of wine and the wind blowing through my hair (no hair jokes please) and the endless rounds of great golf that I thought retirement was all about?

I don't know about you, but I don't want to talk to these medical ologists anymore. I only want to talk to people like geologists, archeologists and other ologists who can teach me how we all got here or how the beautiful sights I'm seeing on my long-planned vacations were formed.

Actually, though there is one ologist I really do want to have more time with—my mix**ologist**. Now he's one ologist I love seeing on a regular basis even though all the other ologists say he's no good for me. What do they know anyway?

OK, we really can't avoid the ologists (also known as doctors), but we *can* decide which one(s) are right for us. And that might not be just because your friend said so.

Let me ask you a question: Have you ever heard anyone say, "Go to my doctor. He's the second best"? Of course not. Everyone thinks their doctor is "the best," but based on what? That's where the work on your part comes in.

You might be surprised to learn this, but outcomes rarely have anything to do with how smart our doctors are, although it helps not to have a dumb doctor. What matters is how caring they are, how familiar they are with you, how willing they are to stop and listen, and most importantly, how in touch they are with your view of what a good outcome for you will be so that they know what is in your best interest.

We all have had doctors, lawyers, accountants, stockbrokers, teachers and others who in some way influenced our lives. Were the best outcomes always from the smartest men or women in the room? More often the best outcomes came when you were clear to them about your needs, your goals, and what you were most interested in accomplishing.

My internist tells me that he is often asked what the best hospital in the area is. His answer? The one closest to you when you need it. In other words, the doctor you choose needs to be the right one for *you,* not the right one for your friend.

"All the good doctors are in New York." It amuses me sometimes when I hear my friends say that "All the good doctors are in New York." It makes me think that knowing how to shovel snow is a prerequisite for being a competent physician. That is just plain silly. If you have a life-threatening condition, you may want to seek out the country's foremost authority on it, but that person could be in Seattle, Chicago or

Valdosta. If your need is for a primary physician or one treating a non-life-threatening one, look closer to home.

Ask your friends for a recommendation, then do your homework. Just because one "best doctor" is a proficient cardiologist doesn't mean he or she should replace your heart valve.

These are the factors I always take into consideration when choosing my ologists (and believe me, I've had plenty of them since I retired for the first time in 2008):

- Board certification in the appropriate specialty
- Currency (are they using the latest knowledge and technology or still stuck in the last century?)
- Personality–do you actually *like* them? Doctor patient communication is enhanced when this sort of synergy exits.
- Willingness to take time to listen. (You might have to "shop" a few doctors to find one who does.)
- Number of patients they treat with whatever the condition is (or in the case of surgery, a high number of that kind of surgery performed annually)
- Legal status. Have they had a lot of lawsuits filed against them? You can usually find this out on state professional licensing websites. (One lawsuit might not concern me that much, depending on what it was. Several would be a red flag.)

We Baby Boomers were taught as children that doctors are "gods." Get over that. Now. They are human beings who have good days and bad days, personal problems and concerns, just like the rest of us.

Doing your homework is important because, guess what they call the person who graduated last in their class at medical school?

Doctor!

The burden of great outcomes depends on you. You must not be a shrinking violet in all things important to you. Step up and shout until you're heard. And if the professional you've chosen can't rise to the occasion, fire them and find another one who will.

Oh, and by the way, I actually did go once to the second best doctor in a specialty I needed, and he really screwed up my shoulder. I've never been the same. Maybe he didn't hear me when I said I wanted to play racquetball again. And I thought he was a good listener.

Chapter Four

We Take Too Many Damn Drugs

Let me set something straight. I'm not anti-doctor and I'm not anti-drug (the legal stuff, of course), but I do worry about how widespread prescription drug use is and how ignorant we often are about using prescribed medications.

Recently I was having dinner with five friends at my country club when, right before ordering, three of them pulled out either a pill bottle or pill box and gulped down God-only-knows-what—without ever missing a beat in the conversation. Two were women, and I noticed them discreetly eyeing each other's ornate pill boxes (the pill popping man was oblivious) and concluded that they were silently assessing who had the more elegant case. I was intrigued that this little ritual was so ingrained among the diners that no one (except me, of course) seemed to think anything of it—beyond the unspoken fashion competition.

Yes, it got me to thinking (again) about something I knew I wanted to cover in this book. I guess you could call it the "responsible way to do drugs."

If you're a Baby Boomer in good health you may not be taking a lot of medications, but your parents probably are and may not be managing those medications very well.

One statistic I saw stated that, on average, Medicare patients who are being discharged from the hospital go home tasked with taking 13—yes, 13—prescription medications. Most likely those 13 aren't prescribed by just one physician, so you can bet that all parties involved don't know the full medication story. It is also a lot of instructions for the patient to understand and follow, so it's not surprising that another study reported that just 47 percent of medications are taken properly by people released from the hospital.

How likely would you be to comply with 13 sets of instructions? I have trouble reading just one set of directions on how to open some of those "hermetically sealed" envelopes that arrive in the mail every week.

When multiple doctors are ordering prescriptions, who's there to make sure there are no dangerous interactions taking place?

You can't count on your doctor or the nurse to do this. They may not be aware of every single medication you're taking, or they may be very busy and don't think about it or they just give you a cursory opinion.

To be safe, this is where your pharmacist comes in. I think pharmacists are an underutilized resource. They will, for free, tell you everything you need to know about your medications. In certain situations, that service could help save your health and maybe even your life.

If you or your parents are taking several medications, it's time to make a field trip to the drug store, no permission slip required. Place everything in a bag (including non-prescriptions medications, vitamins and supplements), walk up to the counter and ask the pharmacist to do a "medication reconciliation." This process is designed to determine if there are potential dangerous interactions among the medications or if there is additional information available to help those medications be consumed safely or more effectively.

So let's have a chat about safe medicating.

We've had clients of our agency who were taking Lipitor in the morning and Crestor in the afternoon. These are both statin drugs and there would never, ever, be a reason to be taking both at the same time.

Years ago I remember looking inside my mother's medicine cabinet and discovering to my horror that she had pills in their original bottles dating back ten years!

"Why do you still have these?" I asked her. "Scott, you never know when you might need them."

Oh, boy. Not only was she putting herself at risk by being her own prescribing physician, but anything she took would be way beyond expired, more like prehistoric. Out they went. She was not amused. Too bad, Mom.

So, let's have a little chat about safe medicating. It won't be as interesting as a chat about safe sex, but it can be just as important for your health.

Follow and understand the directions

This sounds like it's a joke, but researcher Dr. Michael Wolf at Chicago's Feinberg School of Medicine reported reading about a patient's confusion in a pharmacist's log from the 1890s, housed at the Smithsonian National Museum of American History. When instructed to "Shake well," the patient asked, "Does that mean I shake myself?"

A lot of time has passed since that log entry was made, but people still get confused about how to comply with medication instructions. According to Wolf's published study, the more medications a patient takes, the more likely he or she is to misinterpret the directions.

Here are some examples that can be open to interpretation. I'm sure you've encountered these more than once.

Take two pills twice a day

Does this literally mean every 12 hours, or can you take them twice during your waking hours?

Do you take two pills each time or one pill two times?

Take every six hours

Does this mean you need to wake yourself up during the night or can you go eight hours between two of the doses?

Take on an empty stomach

How do you know if your stomach is empty?

How many hours after a meal can you take it?

Do not operate machinery while taking this drug

Does that mean you can't drive?

If there is any doubt whatsoever about what the instructions mean, find out from the doctor or pharmacist —and be careful.

Not long ago I had been taking two Tylenols every four hours for some back pain and decided to try Motrin. I didn't bother to read the label before downing two Motrins and bounding out the door. Later that day when I got home and slowed down enough catch my breath, I read the label and discovered a goof. You only take one Motrin at a time. It's not the same medication. Never assume.

And finally, do not get the mindset that if one is good, two are better. Directions are there for a reason. Don't think you know better than the person who wrote them.

Avoid taking other people's medications

I will start by tattling on myself with an admonishment to "Do as I say, don't do as I do."

One day I was at the golf course and commented to a friend that I was experiencing shoulder pain. He said, "Here, take a couple of my muscle relaxers."

Being the guru of good sense and a bastion of intelligent advice-giving, guess what I did. I said, "Thanks, Jim," and gulped one down, sticking the other in my pocket for later.

"Here, take a couple of my muscle relaxers."

Luckily I lived to tell about it, but I knew in the back of my mind that I was putting myself at risk. I happen to know that the type of medication doctors typically prescribe for toenail fungus can damage my liver because I have high liver enzymes. I'd never take that medication, but I had no idea if any underlying condition of mine might have been exacerbated by a muscle relaxant. I could have endangered myself, so don't do what I did. It's not worth the risk.

Don't assume that over-the-counter medications are harmless

A lot of people don't realize that taking too much Tylenol can cause serious liver damage (NOTE: please reference the warning label on the packaging). Just because you don't need a prescription for a medication doesn't mean it's harmless. All medications (and even supplements like vitamins) can be harmful if taken inappropriately. Don't be your own doctor.

Make sure you are able to identify possible side effects and that you know what to do about them

Some side effects are "mild" and go away. Others are a signal that the drug is wrong for you and require a call or visit to the doctor. Learn in advance what to look for.

Tell your doctor everything about your medications

Even if it's vitamins and supplements, the doctor needs to know. The best thing you can do is give the doctor a list of all your medications, dosages and instructions. Bring the bottles along at the time of your visit for verification.

You don't get a pass on this advice just because electronic medical records are becoming more the norm. They're not foolproof. Especially not yet. First, they may not have notations about over-the-counter medications you are taking. There can be human error, not all your records may have been entered yet and if you order any of your medications from a foreign pharmacy, they won't show up.

Oh, and back to taking too many damn drugs.

As sophisticated as you are, remember that pharmaceutical companies advertise heavily to the general public in order to worry you that you might have a certain illness or condition and prompt you to go see your doctor and ask for their product (depression, "low T," impotence).

While I'm not a doctor, I would think twice about running to the doctor every time I sneeze, demanding a prescription cure. The vast majority of minor illnesses clear up on their own. Unless you are experiencing severe pain or a disturbing symptom like fainting, shortness of breath or chest pain (or anything else a prudent person would figure out is way beyond normal), give it a while. Many doctors feel compelled to write a prescription, even if you don't need it, and that's contributing, in my opinion, to Americans taking too many damn drugs.

Chapter Five

80 in the Left Lane Going 20

My best friend Marty still cringes when he remembers the night three years ago when his father picked him up from the Ft. Lauderdale airport and drove 30 miles on I-95 to his condo in Boynton Beach.

Here's how he describes it:

"Pop cautiously entered the freeway going 20 mph with no concern for the fact that the cars in that lane were going 55. The guy right behind us had to slam on his brakes to keep from hitting us, and when he went around, he showed us with a creative gesture just how much he appreciated our contribution to the enjoyment of his journey. Pop stayed in the right lane for a while (sort of) before drifting into the far left lane with a mere glance in his rearview mirror. He remained in the left lane most of the way to Boynton Beach at the breakneck speed of 45 while frustrated and rushed drivers ping ponged around him. He missed the exit, and we nearly got rear-ended when he suddenly crossed two lanes and slammed on his brakes in a valiant, yet failed, effort to correct his course. By then I was drenched and swimming in a puddle of sweat. After getting off at the next exit uneventfully, I convinced him not to get back on the freeway, and we took the slow way to his house. While we waited at a traffic light he said, 'I sure don't see as well at night as I used to.' You think?! He pulled into the parking lot at his complex, parked three-fifths of the car in one parking spot and two-fifths in the one next to it, and turned off the ignition. I opened the trunk to get my luggage, walked through my father's front door, set my bag down, turned to my father and said, 'Pop, give me the keys. You are never driving again.'"

> **He parked three-fifths of his car in one spot and two-fifths in the one next to it.**

Can you guess how Marty's father responded?

If you answered "not well," you win the seven-day all-expense-paid vacation to Hawaii. Of course it didn't go well, for several reasons.

First, Marty's father's manhood was attached to those car keys, and he wasn't going to give them up without a fight. Also, Marty hadn't thought out well–or at all, really–how to broach the subject so his father wouldn't be defensive. Marty spoke impulsively because he was still getting over nearly being killed six times in 45 minutes. Marty didn't give his father any reason for the demand (you can't assume his father knew how badly he was driving) nor did he offer him any solutions. Oh, and Marty's father, a widower, was a hot commodity at his condo who was still driving at night (though he shouldn't have been) and squiring all the widows around to early bird specials and bingo games.

When you're an elderly man who drives at night you are the ultimate catch regardless of what you look like. It's "Come on down! The price is right!"

You really can't blame Marty for the way he handled the situation. After all, there's no instruction manual for what to do when you believe your parent needs to stop driving. Without a doubt, the "keys" discussion is one of the most difficult ones you can have with a parent.

One thing that makes it difficult is that you have to balance your parent's right to independence—which is hugely important—with your obligation not to let your parent be a menace to public safety.

Here are some startling statistics: 18 percent of pedestrian fatalities are caused by seniors, and 13 percent of vehicle occupancy fatalities are caused by seniors. In other words, this is a real problem, and at some point in time, if a person lives long enough, it must be addressed.

You will probably have to wrestle with some doubts about whether taking the keys away is appropriate yet. Might you be overreacting? Is it possible that just because Mom doesn't drive like she used to she still is driving well enough to be on the road?

You likely have a legitimate concern if you observe some of the following:

- Abrupt lane changes and braking
- Inconsistent acceleration
- Getting lost
- Impaired range of motion that prevents their head or shoulders from turning
- Getting traffic tickets or warnings
- Having frequent fender benders
- Not using turn signals or driving with turn signals flashing (in Florida, we see people every day making right turns from the left lane with their left blinker flashing, or vice versa)
- Poor night driving
- Fear of driving fast on roads like freeways which require speed to be safe
- Running over curbs
- Nearly hitting pedestrians
- Missing turns
- Trouble reading road signs
- Scrapes or dents on the car or mailbox
- Inability to read or follow driving directions
- Impaired peripheral vision
- Hearing loss

- Cognitive decline, including trouble learning new things

If enough of those warning signs are setting off the alarm bells in your head and you feel you must take action, what do you do?

It's never cut and dried. I wish it were.

One of the first things to do is conduct an inventory of all the medications your parent is taking, then contact their doctor's office. Are they taking something that could be impairing their driving ability? If so, find out if there is a substitute for that medication that won't have the same side effect. Sometimes simply changing a medication or changing when the medication is taken can improve a person's competence behind the wheel. If not, then the decision gets tougher.

Keep in mind that with the exception of extreme cases, like the person too impaired by medication or suffering from too much cognitive decline to operate a deadly machine, taking away the keys needs to be gradual, done in gentle steps. It might, in fact, not even be necessary if you can negotiate some compromises.

> **Without a doubt, the "keys" discussion is one of the most difficult.**

Taking away the keys is tantamount to yanking away a person's independence and is likely to be viewed by your parent as the last stop on the train that is whisking them toward the nursing home station. It's a massively complex situation, and you need to be reasonable about it.

Approach the topic with concern and compassion. You might say, "Mom, I worry about what might happen to you behind the wheel. I have noticed that you aren't driving as well as you used to. I can't bear to think of you being a statistic." Tone of voice and attitude are extremely important. If you are accusatory or critical, your parent is likely to become defensive, will probably dig in and you'll find yourself running into a big psychic "STOP" sign.

Be prepared with some ideas that are not as drastic as taking away the keys but which will nonetheless be safer.

These might include an agreement that your parent won't drive at night anymore or will stay within a five-mile radius or won't drive on the freeway. You can get your parent a car with a backup camera.

If it's an emergency situation like my friend Marty faced and you simply cannot let your parent continue to drive, bring a lifeboat to the table. You can't drill a hole in their boat and stand by passively as the life as they know it sinks into the depths of the ocean. This will only contribute to their becoming isolated and increase the chance they will say no.

Alternatives are, unfortunately, not that plentiful in this country unless you live in a large urban area with good public transportation. You will need to be creative.

Offer to drive your parent around to do errands like grocery shopping and hair appointments or find someone who can. Inquire about transportation options from your local senior center. Some communities have transportation services for the elderly. Enlist a friend of your parent who you know is a good driver to pick up the slack. You may also need the help of a trusted friend to help you convince your parent that a change is needed.

Keep this other thing in mind. You cannot *make* your parent give up driving. Your parent is not your child, or anyone's child.

There are, however, people who *can* make them give it up if they truly are a menace on the road. Those people include your parent's physician and people who work for government agencies. In Florida that is the

13 percent of vehicle occupancy fatalities are caused by seniors.

Florida Department of Motor Vehicles (though I strongly suggest keeping the government out of your life and that of your parent in all but the most extreme cases).

A guest on my radio show told me about an elderly couple that I think I would have seriously considered reporting. They arrived at the front desk of a non-profit organization asking for a form to fill out to become volunteers. They said they needed help filling it out because their vision was too bad for them to read what was on the paper. The person behind the desk asked, "How did you get here?" and they responded that they drove!

I am sorry to say that that sort of thing, sadly, just isn't that unusual–and especially here in Florida. I hope everyone wears their seatbelt.

P.S.–Don't forget, there might be a spare set of keys you don't know about. In Marty's father's case, they found the extra set early and after much negotiation, his father did stop driving. All's well that ends well.

Chapter Six

What the Hell is an ADL?
Understanding Your Long-Term Care
Insurance

After rapping loudly on the door I walked into Louise's condo. I had stopped by in response to a call from her daughter who was concerned that Louise, who was hard of hearing, had reached a point of needing some extra help taking care of herself. Louise wasn't bathing regularly anymore, and she was losing control of her bladder more and more often.

Louise and I had spoken on the phone, and she was expecting me. She looked up from her newspaper and said with a serious expression, "You must be Scott."

"I am," I responded, carefully yelling as quietly as possible – if it's possible to yell quietly – so as not to sound unfriendly.

"And you must be Louise. How are you, Louise?"

"Just fine," she replied, as she set her newspaper down on an enormous pile of other newspapers that must have been living in that spot since 1992.

"Louise," I added sternly. "You are *not* fine, and this has to be the last time you ever say that."

She looked at me like I was speaking Martian. I had expected that.

> **"You are *not* 'fine.'"**

"Why can't I ever say that again?" she asked with both curiosity and irritation in her voice. She wasn't all that thrilled to have finally acknowledged that she needed assistance from an agency, and speaking nonsense to her didn't help things.

"Because," I responded, "if you're 'fine' your long-term care insurance won't pay for you to get the help you need that will help make your life around here a little easier."

Fortunately for Louise, she and her late husband Phillip had taken out long-term care insurance, and now that Louise was having trouble with some "activities of daily living," it was time to take advantage of it. Getting the most out of it required being honest about her condition so that all the pieces would fall neatly into place–and that meant not saying she was "fine" when she wasn't.

What exactly is long-term care insurance?

Long-term care insurance is insurance that helps pay for long-term care in your home (or in some cases and states in independent or assisted living communities) should you become ill, temporarily or permanently. This care can be medical in nature, such as nursing visits, but is more often for non-medical needs such as bathing or eating.

Although policies are all different, in most cases to receive benefits the patient must be unable to independently accomplish a minimum of two of five common "activities of daily living." These include: bathing, dressing, eating, toileting and transferring (getting from place to place such as from the bed to the bathroom).

According to the U.S. Department of Health and Human Services, 9 million Americans over the age of 65 currently need long-term care. That statistic is predicted to catapult to 12 million by the year 2020, and most will be cared for at home by family and friends.

Caring for a loved one can be debilitating, and here's a scary fact: 64 percent of family caregivers will pre-decease a loved one they're caring for who has dementia if they don't get outside help.

Buying long-term care insurance makes it possible for the caregiver to have access to the kind of respite care that will improve the quality of their life—and quite possibly extend it. It also ensures that the patient will get help sooner, because somebody else is paying for it, which can help lengthen the life of your loved one.

Whaaatt??? Doesn't Medicare or Medicaid pay for this?

No, it doesn't, although there are state-specific exceptions for Medicaid (check your state regulations). And that's a common misconception. So let's get down to business.

I'm writing this chapter with both you, the Baby Boomer, and your parent in mind.

Let's start with Mom and Dad.

First of all, do you know if your parents have long-term care insurance?

If they have it, do you know what it covers and doesn't cover, when it kicks in and if it's paid up and current?

If you can't answer those questions, you need to get the answers. Today would be a good time to do it. Yesterday would be even better.

I can't tell you how often I speak with the children of our clients who have only a "vague" idea that there might be such a policy in existence, but they aren't sure and don't know where to start looking for it. Don't wait until there's a crisis before finding this out. Being ignorant could cost the family thousands of dollars in the case of a chronic illness. Full-time custodial care can cost as much as $80,000 a year and more. If your parents paid for it and need it, use it!

Now let's talk about you.

Should you buy long-term care insurance?

For most people, the answer is "yes" for the reasons I talked about above, but it's not appropriate for everyone.

The reason I say "yes" for most people is that the odds are not in your favor. According to the non-profit LIFE Foundation (www.lifehappens.org) there's about a 70 percent chance you'll need some type of long-term care after age 65.

Like everything else ... Be a good consumer

Unfortunately, not everyone can afford long-term care insurance, because it is expensive. Like all other insurance, the younger you are when you buy it, the cheaper it is.

Long-term care insurance doesn't make sense for people with significant means who could easily spend $80,000 a year and not miss it. It's not likely to be a priority, either, for people with "big" lifestyles, like travel and expensive cars. Those expenses would go away in the face of a serious illness, and the funds could then be diverted to long-term care.

Like everything else you spend money on, you need to be a good consumer. Do your homework. I always advise people to "buy insurance, not be sold insurance."

Before buying, here is an informative list of things to know and do, offered by the Texas Long-Term Care Partnership:

- Although it may be difficult, try to anticipate what services you might need in the future and choose a policy that's right for you. Creating your plan prior to shopping will help you identify and better understand your needs.

- Prices can vary substantially from one company to another, even for policies with similar benefits. Get quotes from several companies before buying a policy. A company's financial rating by an independent rating service is a helpful indication of the company's overall financial strength.

- The number of consumer complaints against a company is a good indication of the company's customer service record. Your family and friends can be a great source of information about a company's customer service, so be sure to ask them if they've had any experience with the companies you're considering.

- Licensed companies belong to a guaranty association that will pay your claim if your insurance company goes broke. If you buy from an unlicensed company and have a claim, it might go unpaid.

- While past increases are not a guarantee or predictor of future increases, you may want to take the rate history into consideration.

- If you buy insurance through the mail or by phone, ask whether the company has a local agent or a toll-free number you can call if you have questions.

• Because of the many variations in long-term care policies, having an agent with knowledge and experience can help you choose the right coverage for your needs.

• Find out if the insurance companies must give you at least 30 days to look over your long-term care policy after you receive it. Read the policy carefully to be sure it has the benefits and features you want. If you decide to return the policy within the 30 days, you will get a full refund of any premium paid if this law is in effect in your state. It's a good idea to use certified mail so you will have proof that you returned the policy. Be sure to keep a copy of everything you return.

Before making a decision on any one particular policy, be sure you understand all the terms and conditions. Below is a short primer, courtesy of LIFE, on what you absolutely *must* know in order to understand what you are getting:

Benefit Amount and Duration

Most long-term care policies are set up as indemnity plans, which means they pay a fixed dollar amount for each day you receive care. Policyholders usually have a choice of daily benefit amounts ranging from $50 to $300 or more, and can also choose the length of time that benefits will be paid. Long-term care policies generally limit benefits to a maximum dollar amount or a maximum number of days and may have separate benefit limits for nursing home, assisted living community, and home health care within the same policy. For example, a policy may offer

$100 per day up to five years of nursing home coverage (many policies now offer lifetime nursing home coverage) and only up to $80 per day up to five years of assisted living and home health care coverage.

Elimination or Deductible Periods

These terms refer to how many days you must pay out-of-pocket for services that would otherwise be covered before benefits kick in. Most policies offer a choice of deductible from zero to 100 days. The longer the elimination or deductible period, the lower the premium.

Exclusions

When you apply for a policy, you'll be asked to fill out a medical questionnaire, and probably undergo a checkup with a doctor. This helps the insurance company find out about any existing health issues (known as preexisting conditions) that make it more likely that you'll one day need long-term care. Preexisting conditions may make coverage more expensive, and the insurance company may choose not to cover you for these conditions during your first six months of coverage.

Inflation Protection

Because long-term care prices are rising steadily, the benefit you buy today may be inadequate tomorrow. By purchasing inflation protection, your policy benefit will automatically increase each year at a specified rate (such as 5 percent) compounded over the life of the policy.

Nonforfeiture Benefits

This feature allows you to drop your coverage and still receive a portion of the benefits. Nonforfeiture benefits may be received two ways, depending on the policy and option you choose. Return of premium provides a cash payment that is a percentage of the total premiums you have paid. With a shortened benefit period, you still receive coverage after you've stopped paying, but with a reduced benefit period or amount.

Renewability

Almost all long-term care policies are guaranteed renewable. That means that they cannot be canceled as long as you pay your premiums. However, companies can raise premiums as long as they raise them for an entire class of policyholders. The renewability provision, usually found on the first page of the policy, outlines under what conditions the company can cancel the policy or raise premiums.

Waiver of Premium

This provision allows you to stop paying premiums while you are receiving benefits. Your policy may contain restrictions on this feature, such as requiring you to receive care for a certain number of days or sessions before premiums are waived.

But wait. There's more (that you need to know)!

To get long-term care benefits, you have to have a care plan prepared by a nurse or social worker. Often the doctor has to state that the patient needs help with activities of daily living.

Some policies have a "restoration clause" that allows your benefits to "re-set," even after having used some of them. An example might be when you use some benefits while recovering from hip surgery. After a pre-determined period, such as six months, the full benefit you contracted for is restored.

And here's one more list—some questions you need to ask before signing on the dotted line:

- How much is the daily benefit?
- Will the payments remain "level?" (Be the same for the duration of the policy.)
- What levels of care does the policy cover and to what extent? Does it cover home health, all levels of nursing home care and custodial care?
- How long must I pay out of my own pocket (elimination period) before I can start receiving benefits?
- How much is the deductible?
- What are the term limits? In other words, what is the dollar limit, the day limit, the year limit?
- Does the policy cover dementia?

- Am I protected against inflation?
- Can I pay a family member to care for me?
- Will the policy pay for a "private" caregiver (someone who isn't certified and/or licensed)?

Using the Benefits

When the time comes to use the benefits, as I said earlier, I suggest you use them sooner rather than later, as this makes life easier for everyone. Many people worry about "using them up" too soon. Without them, the family *caregiver* is likely to get "used up too soon."

I also strongly recommend that you get professional help to apply for the benefits. Home healthcare agencies such as mine have people on staff who know how to do this correctly. Making even one mistake can delay the start of benefits by weeks or even months.

Chapter Seven

Caregiver Roulette

The telephone rang one afternoon and the man on the other end of the line said, "My mother is recovering from a broken hip. She's going to need full-time home health-care for a few months. I want you to send me your best caregiver."

"Thank God you called when you did," I responded. "My best caregiver has been sitting on a shelf for weeks in my office just waiting for your call."

Well, the truth is I said no such thing, but I thought it.

That sort of request is, frankly, ridiculous. The question he should have asked is how do you hire your caregivers? My "best" caregiver is working. So is my second best and likely my third and fourth, too, unless their client passed away yesterday. If they aren't a high quality, credentialed and professional aide, they won't be working for us in the first place.

That can't be said for all agencies, which is why it's important to carefully check out any agency you are considering hiring. Beware of those with a 65-step hiring process—if the person can walk 65 steps from their car to the office, they're hired. That sort of agency is likely to send out the first warm body they can reach regardless of how qualified or appropriate the caregiver is, and you are left watching the "caregiver roulette" wheel spin. The odds of that match-up being a winner are stacked against you.

"Send me your best caregiver."

Getting back to my story, you need to be aware that there isn't ever one "best" caregiver, but there is likely to be one "best" caregiver (or two) *for any given client*. Like any relationship, many factors go into making a match, and it's far more than the spin of a wheel. What works for one person doesn't work for another, and what makes it work isn't always obvious. The time and attention a good agency spends on this significantly increases your odds of winning at the caregiver roulette game.

Here's one example: Last year a daughter called us to hire a caregiver for her 90-year-old mother who seemed to have given up on life. She and her siblings who lived out of state were all delightful and devoted and, I'm sure, thought they were doing the right thing by insisting the caregiver provided be a woman in her fifties – or older.

Their logic was that there would be a better chance their mother could relate if they were closer in age.

I didn't agree with their thinking and, instead, sent them a 19-year-old nursing student named "Ashley." My gut feeling, honed by my experience in the field, told me that Ashley, who was loaded with personality and enthusiasm for her job, would be the perfect choice.

They were horrified.

Simply horrified.

At first.

> **The important thing is to know who you are doing business with.**

But then, guess what? ... Ashley and the client fell in love with each other! Ashley became the "local" granddaughter the woman wanted, and in very short order our client had come out of her shell. She called me one day to thank me for choosing Ashley for her. She said Ashley had changed her life. Had I let the daughter choose the caregiver, she would have probably chosen someone much older, and the outcome would have been quite different.

And that brings me to the idea about interviewing potential caregivers that come from an agency. "Can I interview the person beforehand?" is one of the most common questions I hear.

What I'm going to say about that will probably surprise you: If you are working with an agency you trust, don't bother interviewing a potential aide. There is *no difference* in the success rate of the client/caregiver choice when the caregiver is interviewed by family members and when she or he is not interviewed by them.

Really? You might be asking.

Yes. Really.

Family members interview from the perspective of their own mindset, not the loved one's mindset. They might choose someone because *they* are comfortable with that person, which is no guarantee their loved one will feel the same way. The candidate might be the best communicator in the world in an interview, but that doesn't necessarily make that person the best caregiver in that situation.

The only way to find out if it's going to work out is to try it and see. Kind of like dating.

There *is* one interview that should be at the top of your list, however, and that is the one you do with potential agencies. The important thing is to know who you are doing business with. Once you have confidence in the agency, butt out and let them do the choosing for you. It is, after all, what they do every single day. They are going to have a far better feel for the right person than you are. (Sorry, I don't want to hurt your feelings, but it happens to be true.)

Here's a little anecdote about a man who asked a home healthcare agency to send someone to his home. After just one day of caring for his wife, who had had elective surgery and couldn't yet fend for herself, he knew caregiving wasn't for him. He was both relieved and nervous about bringing a total stranger into the house, but he was willing to trust the agency and give it a shot. The caregiver turned out to be just what the doctor ordered, and they all lived happily ever after...or something like that.

Oh, yes. I forgot to mention that that man was me, and I had instructed my agency not to tell me who was coming and not to tell the caregiver who came who I was. It's not uncommon for people who work for my agency not to know me because I'm not in the office much, and I figured it would make her nervous if she knew.

Not all home health agencies are alike.

The reason I'm telling you this story is that I want you to know that I know how it feels to be bringing a stranger into the mix when someone you love needs help. But I also want to stress that I did so with the greatest possible confidence not simply because I own the company but because my home health agency conducts business the way it should be conducted to ensure success (and improve the roulette odds).

Just as not all restaurants, attorneys, grocery stores and hair salons are alike, the same goes for home health agencies. You need to do some significant homework before settling on the one you are going to trust your beloved family member to.

You can ask for references if you're so inclined, but HIPAA (privacy) regulations make it unlikely you'll get any. Don't be fooled by fancy websites, glitzy TV commercials or pretty pictures in a brochure. Instead, seek referrals from doctors, hospitals, rehabilitation centers, elder agencies, trusted professionals such as attorneys, and friends.

In preparation, investigate at least three agencies, getting answers to the following questions:

- How long have you been in business?
- Is your agency willing to provide another caregiver if the first one doesn't work out"? (Unless you're me, you don't marry the first person you date.)
- Do clients have access to a live person 24/7 if there's a problem or emergency?
- How do you verify the employees' credentials such as citizenship, driver's license and auto insurance?
- Do you conduct a background check?
- What does the agency do if the person cannot make their shift? Do you have a competent fallback person?
- Are your caregivers bonded and insured?
- Do your caregivers receive regular training to stay updated? (My agency has an online university. If a caregiver needs more training to deal with a client with a certain condition, they can log on and learn more about it.)
- Do your aides speak understandable English?
- Is the owner involved?

At the end of the day it's a gut feeling about the agency you hire–after you do your due diligence.

I'm a strong believer in choosing franchised agencies rather than independent ones because franchisees have a considerable amount of oversight and can lose their franchise if the business isn't being properly run.

Oh, and here's one more extremely important thing to tell you.

What's more frightening than your ailing parent falling and getting hurt? The caregiver who isn't an employee of a home healthcare agency falling and getting hurt.

I strongly advise against finding your caregiver from a nurse registry (or from an independent source like Craigslist). You might be tempted, because the hourly rate is probably going to be less than the rate from a home health agency, but there are (scary) reasons for that.

Caregivers from nurse registries are most often independent contractors, not employees, and this can put you at financial risk.

Independent contractors are unlikely to be bonded and insured. They are unlikely to be covered under workers' compensation. If they have an accident in your house you can be sued, and this is not something normal homeowner's insurance covers.

The registry may not be taking taxes out of their paycheck, and if the person doesn't file his or her taxes, the IRS can come to you with bill in hand. That happened to one of our clients, and it took months to resolve.

Also, independent contractors are supposed to be free to set their own schedules and are expected to be experts. Independent contractors get no supervision, no ongoing training and no one to verify that they are keeping up with their skills. In this environment you are the employer, and it's unlikely that you are able to provide that supervision, training and education.

When hiring a caregiver there are some important things to keep in mind.

These are people, not robots or slaves. They may not do everything exactly the way you think they should be done, so choose your battles. You want to build a partnership, not run a dictatorship. If your caregiver doesn't fix chicken the way you would, let it go.

Chill out if she's watching TV or making a phone call while your mother sleeps. This takes nothing away from your parent's safety or comfort.

If you have a problem with the caregiver, discuss it first with the agency, not the caregiver. (By the way, this is not an option if you are using someone from a registry or someone (who) you have hired privately. You have to deal with it directly in that situation).

And finally, caregivers are precious resources, people who often do things that you can't, won't or don't know how to do. Never lose sight of that fact and remember to say "please" and "thank you."

Typical duties performed by home healthcare aides (state laws may apply):

Light housekeeping

Laundry

Bed linen changes

Meal preparation

Food shopping

Ambulation and transferring

Bathing and dressing assistance

Taking the client to doctor appointments and other activities outside the home serving as a guide, companion or helper

Toileting

Companionship

Checking pulse, temperature and respiration

Helping with simple, prescribed exercises

Medication reminders

Feeding assistance

Using special equipment such as a Hoyer lift

Chapter Eight

Mom Always Loved You More!

My wife Irene and I were enjoying a cocktail and some much-anticipated down time at The Beach Club in Palm Beach one evening around sunset when my cell phone rang. She shot me one of those "Really? You're going to answer it?" looks. "Yes," I reluctantly signaled her, gesturing that I'd make it quick (I'd better—we were overdue for a date night, and if I knew what was good for me, I wouldn't spend my time taking business calls).

"Scott, this is Wendy Matthews," said the pressured voice on the other end. The day before, I had spoken to Wendy about care options for her mother Martha who wasn't doing well at home by herself.

"My brother is going to call you in a few minutes," she said without waiting for me to say hello. "Bill thinks I'm nuts, but he's an ass. Don't listen to anything he tells you to do. I know what's best for Mom. He hardly ever sees her. He just flies in from New York three or four times a year and thinks he can just write a check and make everything all better."

"OK, Wendy," I replied. "Could you please ask him to call me tomorrow?"

It was too late. A call was coming in from area code 212 and I was pretty sure that the caller was Bill.

Shoot, I thought to myself (though that probably wasn't the actual word that popped into my head).

"Wendy, I think he's calling me now.

"Remember, Scott, he's not in charge here. I am."

With an apologetic grimace, I took the next call and, sure enough, it was Bill.

"Scott," said the calm, deep voice on the other line. "I understand that you and Wendy spoke yesterday about options for our mother."

"Yes," I replied.

"Well, keep in mind that Wendy is a bit on the neurotic side. She sees monsters in every closet, if you know what I mean."

Uh, OK, I'm thinking to myself.

"I'm in a much better position to make decisions about our mother. Nothing should be entrusted to Wendy or my other sister. Please consult me before anything is done. OK?"

Other sister? I'm still stuck on that new piece of information.

"All right, Bill. I will get back in touch."

"I'm sorry, Irene," I said with that charming smile that still melts her heart (I hope) after 43 years of marriage. Let the date begin.

The phone rang again. Uh, oh.

By now the figurative daggers were starting to feel more like real ones, so I turned off the ringer and put the phone into my coat pocket.

On the way home I listened to my messages.

> **"He thinks he can just write a check and make everything all better."**

"Scott, this is Kathy Bellinger," the message began. "I'm Martha Keller's daughter. I understand my sister is looking into care options for my mother. Bill and Wendy have ganged up on me all their lives, and I'm concerned they're going to go behind my back and make decisions about my mother that she won't like. I've been the closest one to her, and she told me a long time ago that if anyone ever had to make life or death decisions for her, it should be me. Please call me right away. Any time tonight is fine, even if it's late."

Here we go again, I thought to myself. Another dysfunctional family. Another ping-pong match among siblings with their parent being the ball. Another elderly person who was going to suffer for it.

> **Here we go again .... another dysfunctional family.**

The sad fact is that there is often incredible disagreement among siblings when their parents start needing help and the old wounds from childhood get in the way. It's something people in my business deal with all the time.

Rebecca might not say she's still angry that her sister Bonnie got a more expensive prom dress than she did, but she is. After all, that meant Mom loved Bonnie more. And so the rivalry continues and even escalates with the magnified stress an aging parent can present. The kids are still, after all these years, vying for a parent's love or financial support.

What's needed at a crisis point in a parent's life is good decision-making, which is severely hampered when brothers and sisters can't agree. Often they're disagreeing more because of the relationship they have with each other than what is in the best interest of their parent.

They likely have no expertise in making the kinds of decisions facing them and are doing so based solely on the fact that they hate each other and want to get back at their brother or sister or show them who's boss or who loves their parent more. You get the picture.

There is very little difference between these kinds of squabbles and those that divorced parents have over the children caught in the middle. The well-being of a person whose life hangs in the balance takes a back seat to ego.

A common argument is about whether the parent should stay home. One (usually the brother) wants to write a check, send Mom to a good assisted living community, and go on about his life. His sister, on the other hand, thinks this is cold and unfeeling. "Look at everything Mom sacrificed for you!" A sibling carrying most of the burden of care may get lambasted by a brother or sister for the way that care is being provided and feel unfairly criticized or put upon. One sibling will decide that too much (or too little) is being spent on the parent's care, and a disagreement is born with no good resolution in sight. The number of depressing potential scenarios is endless.

If any of this sounds familiar, I'm not surprised. According to the National Alliance for Caregiving, about 20 million Americans are providing care for a parent or in-law. You might be a participant in one of those family boxing matches right now.

So let me ask you a question: Do you see yourself in any of these toxic types of sibling bad actors?

The Martyr

You stoically trudge along doing what has to be done to take care of Mom or Dad, all the while resenting everyone —and letting them know that you resent them.

The Smart One

You think your way is the best, and you aren't willing to concede that your sibling might be right after all, even now and then.

The Criticizer

You aren't nearly as involved in the care of your parent as your sibling, yet you "Monday morning quarterback" every action and decision your sibling makes.

The "Lawyer"

You argue every single aspect of every single potential option to the point that almost nothing gets done (except arguing).

The Free Spirit

You've spent every dime you ever made, and then some, and are counting on an inheritance to see you through. You don't hang around to do any caregiving, but you don't mind writing yourself a check now and then out of your parent's account.

The Warrior

You have always seen your siblings as adversaries and are primed for battling out every decision until you win.

The Denier

You simply don't believe that your parent is as bad off as your sibling says, and you discount the dire warnings they're giving you.

OK. So now what?

Ahem.....

Time to grow up! OK, so maybe it's not you who's not being the grownup, but that doesn't matter. What *does* matter is that your parent's care will be determined in large part by how well you can get along with your siblings. While I can't fix old wounds (you'll need to consult your therapist for that) I can at least provide some guidelines that might make this situation a bit easier.

• Make up your mind that you are going to do everything in your power to work harmoniously with your sibling(s) and ask that they make the same vow. It is, after all, supposed to be about the well-being of someone you both love.

• Hold a family meeting with the goal of assigning tasks to the person best equipped to do them. One person may be better at sorting out the finances while the other is a better researcher who can find out about care options. One may have more time to spend, while the other may have more money. Both are equally valuable.

- Provide regularly scheduled updates about each other's progress on their tasks. This can be done in person, by phone or via email. When everyone is kept in the loop, there's less opportunity for distrust or misunderstanding.

- Discuss from the very beginning what the expectations are about finances, and who will be in charge. If this seems like an unsolvable bone of contention, enlist the help of an independent third party such as a family friend to bring reason into the mix. If that doesn't work you may need to hire an elder mediator or geriatric care manager.

- Designate one child to be the primary caregiver or major decision-maker where care and medical decisions are concerned, and respect the decisions of that person, even if it's a different decision than one you would make. Be supportive in every possible way of that person.

- Make sure the primary caregiving sibling has an outlet for respite such as help from a part-time paid caregiver. Caring for an elderly person can put significant stress on the caregiver and negatively affect that person's health and well-being.

- Avoid criticizing the caregiver sibling, especially if you aren't down in the trenches with them and may not be seeing the entire picture.

- Ask the caregiving sibling what you can do to help. Listen, then follow through to the best of your ability.

- If possible, figure out a way the caregiving sibling can be financially compensated.

- If you can't agree on the level of care your parent needs, bring in an expert for a professional opinion, such as a geriatric care manager or even someone like us.

- Make sure that your parent is as bad—or as good—as you believe them to be, before trying to force on everyone else your opinion about what should be done.

- Don't be surprised by gender differences when it comes to points of view. In interviews with 149 pairs of siblings, professor of sociology Sarah Matthews at Cleveland State University found that sisters expect siblings to be a cooperating team with a lot of communication. Brothers, on the other hand, are likely to act more independently and may negotiate directly with parents without keeping sisters informed.

- Finally, if your parent is mentally competent—or is not yet at a stage where he or she needs any care —hold a meeting with your parent and siblings and ask what your parent would want should the need for help arise. Write it down. Distribute it to everyone and, as much as possible, stick to your parent's wishes when the time comes.

Chapter Nine

My Parents Are Outliving My Money

Alice did not like her son Frank's fiancée one bit, and she had no problem letting Frank know how she felt. Briana wasn't educated enough. She didn't wear her hair right. She was lazy. She would make a terrible mother, and she had the table manners of a baboon at a tea party.

Oh, and one more thing. Alice let Frank know that if he went through with the marriage, Frank would be written out of her will. Any questions?

You can imagine how damaging this manipulative behavior was to their mother-son relationship. Three years later, Alice, who didn't disinherit Frank after all when he married Briana but did boycott the wedding, found out just how bad it was when she had a stroke and Frank became her guardian.

Because of the hostility he felt, Frank brought in the lowest-paid caregiver he could find, and Alice did not get the kind of care she would have wanted or could afford. Why not? Well, that meant more was left for Frank when she died. Payback. Funny how that works.

Using money as a weapon is as old as money itself, and it doesn't matter if it's old money or new money.

Money can be, in fact, a weapon of family destruction. And that's why it's essential you remove yourself from any sort of gamesmanship like that used by Frank's mother and instead use your time and energy to plan, plan, plan. Way ahead. And let your children know where they stand and what you expect.

Using your money as a weapon against your children will teach them to do the same not only to you but probably with each other as well.

And speaking of "children," to expect that those who have warred with each other all their lives will sit down and have a Kumbaya moment and resolve to work cooperatively for your benefit when you are not at your best is, well, just silly. It's not going to happen.

One may want to spend more of the money while the other wants to spend less. One thinks Dad needs a full-time caregiver. The other thinks Dad's just fine with a little help. It gets very complicated and can morph into a very ugly cocktail.

Even without sibling issues muddying the waters, children are known to make really terrible decisions where their parents are concerned for a multitude of reasons, some wrapped in the pretty paper of good intentions but filled with bloated ignorance, others wrapped in a smelly newspaper of greed like in Frank's situation.

Let's talk for a moment about something parents don't like to think about, or even acknowledge.

Not every child will have their parents' best interests at heart. They may make care (or other spending) decisions based primarily on saving money (more for them later) rather than on what's right for the parent. They may simply be unprepared to make intelligent decisions about their parents' financial or physical well-being, or they might be (to put it indelicately) leeches.

Money can be a weapon of family destruction.

Take the case of Susan, 43. While her brother Will became a successful lawyer, Susan hooked up with several "loser guys" and ended up being a single parent with one year of junior college, a part-time clerical job and living in a cottage on her parents' property.

Will suspected for years that his parents were subsidizing Susan and, in his way of looking at it, enabling her dependency, but there wasn't much he could do about it. When their father died eight years ago, however, Will began to feel very protective of his mother and started paying much closer attention to what was going on. He didn't like one bit what he discovered, but he wasn't surprised.

Their mother was writing Susan checks to the tune of about $10,000 a year, in addition to providing her with free rent and paying for most of her food. Will didn't need the money (so that wasn't the issue) but he worried that if his mother kept writing checks to Susan she would run out of money, and then what would happen? Would Susan get off her behind and get a good job and take care of their mother's financial needs? Will doubted it and stepped in. When the checks stopped, Susan became furious at both her mother and brother, threatened to keep her daughter away from her grandmother if her mother didn't "help her out," and the family dissolved into a million glass shards.

> **Your parents' financial situation is nothing like they expected.**

I believe that the very best thing you can do, and do it now, is meet with an elder law attorney. By planning ahead for every conceivable eventuality, there's a better chance your needs will be met the way you would want if you can no longer handle them yourself. Laying out everything ahead of time can also significantly reduce sibling squabbles as well as opportunities for those closest to you to be tempted to make decisions on your behalf that are not in your best interest.

Let's talk now a little about your parents. If they are like millions of the elderly, their financial situation is nothing like they expected for the following reasons:

They have lived longer than they projected.

Interest rates are far lower than they anticipated, so their cash flow is less.

Everything costs more.

Their home equity has plummeted.

Also like a lot of folks from that generation they have saved their money "for a rainy day." It may be up to you to point out that it's raining and raining hard, and they need to get some help quickly.

Does this cut into your inheritance?

Yes. (But not mine. I inherited the "Greenberg" hundreds without incident).

Should that matter?

I am sure you know the answer to that.

If you're in charge of your parents' money, be positive that you know what you're doing. Make sure you are making spending decisions for the right reasons. Seek expert advice. Don't see your parents' money as your personal cookie jar. I cannot tell you how many people have been deemed ineligible for Medicaid when needing to go into a nursing home because one of their children decided to make themselves a financial gift or two (or three). And in case you're expecting an inheritance, it won't be there if it all goes to a nursing home because Medicaid benefits have been denied since you couldn't wait to get yourself a new car or you used Mom's money to pay for your kids' tuition.

Financial planning of all kinds, including being able to qualify for Medicaid, should be the work of experts. It is not something you should do after reading a few articles on the internet.

Keep in mind that in every family there's the possibility that someone has designs on your (or your parents') money. One out of every five people over the age of 65 will be victimized by some type of fraud, and 79 percent of that fraud comes from trusted family members.

Money makes people do stupid things—and unkind things —and unethical things.

Don't be a pawn in any sort of those things—wittingly or unwittingly.

Don't let money be a weapon of family destruction in your life.

Chapter Ten

What Happens if You Don't Make it Home Tonight?

My seatbelt was fastened and the seatback tray in front of me was in the upright position as the US Airways jet I was on paused on the taxiway at New York's LaGuardia Airport. It was 8:15 a.m., and we were about to take off for Charlotte, North Carolina where I was speaking at a meeting. Little did I realize that at that exact moment a sinister plan was being executed in Boston which would inflict unimaginable evil and terror on the people of the United States. That day was September 11, 2001, and I have never been the same.

The words "There but by the grace of God, go I" never meant more to me than it did after I learned upon landing the full horror of what had occurred, a sentiment that still rattles the deepest parts of my psyche when I think about that awful day.

I flew all over the country for business in those days and I just as easily could have been flying out of Boston headed for Los Angeles on the ill-fated American Airlines jet.

What would have happened if I hadn't made it home that night?

A few years later after moving to Florida and buying the home healthcare company I now own, I attended a seminar on advance directives and planning given by my friend Michelle Hollister, elder law attorney and President of The National Guardianship Association. This is how she began her talk:

What happens if you don't make it home tonight?

Chills ran down my spine. There was that question again.

The room got very quiet as I watched the audience creating silent scenarios in their heads of just what that would mean to themselves and those they love.

How prepared is your family should you suddenly and unexpectedly die? Michelle challenged. What if you weren't killed but were severely injured and couldn't speak for yourself? What if you could never live a normal life again? Would you want to be kept on life support? Would your estate go to the people you wanted it to in the way you would like?

I could see on the attendees' faces that a lot of those questions were ones they not only had never addressed but had probably never even thought about.

90 percent of deaths can be anticipated...10 percent are sudden.

So, let me give you the same challenge.

What happens if you don't come home tonight?

I've discovered that people often believe that a last will and testament is all they need to ensure a smooth and satisfactory transition to those left behind. Nothing could be further from the truth.

A last will and testament is good for a few things including making sure that family heirlooms go to the people you designate and, if you have minor children, designating the person who will care for them if their other parent isn't available. I'm oversimplifying this, of course, to make a point. But the fact is that it doesn't address anything whatsoever pertaining to your affairs if you live but become incompetent or incapacitated. It is not designed to designate specific people to handle your affairs if you do not die or to set up legal entities to protect your assets.

Expecting a will to take care of every wish and eventuality is kind of like expecting a car with one tire to be equipped to take you on a road trip.

I'm not trying to scare you but rather to make you aware that life won't necessarily unfold the way you expect it to.

The good news is that 90 percent of deaths can be anticipated, which means that only 10 percent are sudden or unexpected. The problem is that since you have no way of knowing if you'll be part of the 90 percent or the 10 percent, you're better off preparing for the latter.

In this chapter I'll be outlining the typical documents that well-prepared people make sure to have with the aim of giving themselves and their loved ones peace of mind. Here's my disclaimer first: I am not an attorney, and each person's situation is different, so I am not offering legal advice. This information is here for educational purposes only and you must consult an attorney to determine what is right for you.

Speaking of attorneys, do you know the difference between an elder law attorney and an estate planning attorney? People sometimes think they are the same, but they're not, and here's the distinction I find most useful:

Elder law attorneys specialize in helping you arrange your affairs and anticipate eventualities that are likely for you during your lifetime. This might include setting up a durable power of attorney or living will (to be defined further down in the chapter).

Estate planning attorneys specialize in helping get everything in order that will apply after your death, such as setting up trusts and wills. Again, this is an oversimplification, but I think you get the idea. Notice that I used the word "specialize" where both those types of attorneys are concerned. I encourage you to seek out specialists for these crucial parts of your life and death planning. Just any old attorney won't do. Your son's wife's neighbor's brother might be an excellent personal injury attorney, but he's not likely to be up on the latest laws and regulations pertaining to this type of planning.

> **Do you know the difference between an elder law attorney and an estate planning attorney?**

Why use an attorney when you can get much, if not all, of the documents you might need through an online legal service? Won't an attorney cost more? Yes, it probably will cost more to use an attorney rather than a website, but this can be penny wise and pound foolish. The law is complicated, and the laws of each state vary. Do you really want to take a chance that you might overlook something crucial or make a mistake that would end up not having the outcome for your loved ones that you wanted? Personally I'm not willing to take that risk.

Let's talk now about common important documents (not all documents are needed by all people. It depends on your situation).

Last Will and Testament

Wikipedia defines a last will and testament as "a legal declaration by which a person, the testator, names one or more persons to manage his or her estate and provides for the distribution of his property at death." Anyone with any assets at all, such as a bank account or home, most likely needs a will.

Let me ask you this. If you have a will, when was the last time you looked at it? If it's been more than three years there's a good chance something has changed in your life that requires a change in your will. Maybe your minor children have come of age or you got divorced or your son ran away to Kurdistan with an exotic girl who doesn't speak English but knows 50 ways to spend his money. Don't lock it away and forget about it. Dust off those cobwebs and take a fresh look.

Living Will

This document specifies whether or not you want to prolong medical treatments in the event that you contract a terminal illness or are in a permanent vegetative state. This directive is not instituted until and unless you are incapacitated and often can only be applied after certification by a doctor or other professional (depending on the laws of your state) that your illness or incapacity is permanent.

DNR

A DNR (Do Not Resuscitate) is a legal order written either by a hospital or other legal entity which states the patient's desire not to undergo any advanced or "heroic" lifesaving measures such as CPR in the event the patient's heart stops or the patient stops breathing. You can't just tell a paramedic or emergency room doctor that the patient has a DNR. Unless you show it to them, lifesaving measures will be taken.

P.O.L.S.T.

This is an acronym for Physician's Orders for Life-Sustaining Treatment. P.O.L.S.T. is not an option in all states and may be called something different in your state (it's called M.O.L.S.T. in New York). The idea behind it is to be more specific about what kind of treatment you want in a situation where you are gravely ill or injured. A DNR order only applies if the heart or breathing has stopped. A P.O.L.S.T., usually prepared by a doctor, can address certain situations such as whether you would want a feeding tube inserted or an infection treated. It is generally of interest to someone with a serious illness or who is very sick. It covers more specifics than a living will, which can be too vague to ensure your wishes.

Power of Attorney

This is a document which allows another person to represent you in legal or financial matters. An example would be someone going to the closing of a real estate purchase and signing for it on your behalf. A regular power of attorney only applies for some particular circumstance or limited time while you are competent. If you die or become incompetent, the power of attorney is negated.

Durable Power of Attorney

This document allows someone to act on your behalf. I have seen unfortunate situations where someone gets dementia and hasn't signed a durable power of attorney, thus tying the hands of their spouse who needs to sell their jointly owned house or cash in jointly owned stocks and cannot do it.

I cannot stress how important it is for you to know the laws of your state before having such a document executed, however. In the State of Florida, a DPOA becomes effective as soon as it is signed, whether you have been declared incompetent or not. If the person you designate is a nefarious character, the DPOA could be abused even if you're perfectly in control. If that happens, you can kiss your money good-bye.

Trust

A trust allows a third party, called a trustee, to hold onto assets on behalf of beneficiaries. Trusts can be designed many different ways depending on exactly how and when you want your assets to pass to beneficiaries. Because trusts usually avoid probate, assets can pass more quickly to beneficiaries than they might if specified in a will, which can end up in court. It can also help reduce or avoid taxation.

Healthcare Surrogate

This document appoints someone to make medical decisions for you if you are unable to do so. It also allows the doctor to talk to your designated friend or family member about your condition.

People are often surprised to learn that doctors cannot talk to them about their spouse's condition (or their adult child's condition) without that person's permission. It gets even more complicated with domestic partners. Without a healthcare surrogate document, you might not even be able to get into the intensive care unit to see your loved one if you are unmarried and are not that person's healthcare surrogate.

I cannot stress enough how important it is for you to tell the people closest to you what documents and orders you have and where to find them. Your family needs to know ahead of time what your wishes are so that there is less confusion during a crisis.

"What do you mean you can't talk to me? I'm his wife."

Do not keep sole copies of your important papers in a safety deposit box in case they are needed on a Friday night of a holiday weekend and the next time the bank is open is Tuesday morning. If one of those documents is a DNR and you are terminally ill, it won't do you any good in the bank vault. My wife and I each have a flash drive with all our important documents on them that we carry in our wallets.

When delegating who is to take care of what, think about what each interested party does best, and put it in writing that that's their job. One child might be better at making medical decisions while the other would do a better job handling finances.

Craft your paperwork to allow you to be in control for as long as possible. Be careful not to give it up too soon. The irony is that by doing this in advance it allows you to be in control even though you are no longer in control.

Don't delay in taking care of this. Now is the time when your mind is clear and there's little chance someone is coercing you into something that might not be in your best interest.

Keep in mind that getting these documents done is as much for the people in your life that you love as it is for yourself. It allows you to be taken care of the way you want and allows your loved ones to just be there with you and for you when their presence is what you need the most. With your wishes documented, the decisions that need to be made are clearer and easier.

I have no idea if I will come home tonight or not, but one thing I do know is that if I don't, everything that could possibly be anticipated and put in writing where my wife and I are concerned has been done. And that's how I show my family that I love them.

Chapter Eleven

Smart Phones Make Me Feel Dumb

"Help! I've fallen and I can't get up!" has to be one of the corniest lines ever written for a TV commercial–but it's also one of the most memorable and parodied lines in advertising history. Even though the ad first aired in 1987, people who weren't even born then have incorporated it into their lexicon. Comedians use it to this day to summon a laugh from audiences.

Well, that venerable piece of electronic equipment isn't your grandfather's Life Alert® anymore. No sir-ee. It's still around, but thanks to advances in the technology, if "Mrs. Fletcher" falls now, can't get up and can't push the button, the Life Alert's® fall detection system will make the call for her.

And I think that's a good thing.

But I'm not too sure about some of the other technology redefining our lives. In case you hadn't noticed I'm a pretty opinionated guy, but when it comes to technology I am both in awe of all the amazing inventions already here and coming our way, and scared to death of them at the same time. (Nothing makes me feel dumber than my "smart" phone.)

What does technology mean for us? On the plus side, it can help my children know where I am, but I have to ask myself, do I want my children knowing where I am? It can tell my wife how many times I opened the refrigerator today, but do I really want her to start interrogating me about how many snacks I ate when she wasn't looking?

I could put a tracking device on my dentures if I had them and I'd never lose them again but, hey, that would be just plain creepy.

Twenty or 25 years ago I read an article in the *New York Times* called "The Electric Fork" which posed the question: Just because you can make an electric fork, should you? With that in mind I think we need to carefully evaluate whether the latest bell and whistle device is going to simplify or complicate our life, whether its benefits outweigh the almost certain aggravation and frustration of making it work the way it's supposed to and whether it became a product merely because it was possible to make it. Sometimes the traditional way is just as good or better.

But let me get off my soap box for a minute and talk about the cool stuff.

Let's begin with the electric fork. Yes. There really is one that vibrates when you eat too fast. It's supposed to keep you from overeating by slowing you down until the food you've shoved in your mouth makes it to your stomach. That's probably not on my bucket list.

A lot of folks keep in touch with their children and grandchildren via Skype®, which sure beats the old days when you had to wait until the long distance calling rates went down on Saturday afternoon so you could afford to talk longer than the duration of a Life Alert® commercial.

You can get a pill box that sounds a quiet alarm when it's time to take your pill. If you don't take it, the alarm gets progressively louder until you do. If you don't take it after a certain period of time it will send an electronic message to someone you designate who can nag you the old fashioned way.

> **I could put a tracking device on my dentures.**

There are sensors that tell you how many times you got out of bed during the night, apps for how many steps you took during the day and how many calories you ate, and devices you can hook up to your smart phone to help you monitor your blood pressure at any given moment.

Going to the bathroom at night can be safer than ever thanks to sensors that turn on a dim light when you enter the room and a toilet seat that lights up so you don't miss. (I bet my wife would like me to have one of those.) Homes can have shelves installed that come down to you from above or up to you from below at the touch of a button, which can keep you off the floor and not needing Mrs. Fletcher's magic button.

You can make a phone call from your wristwatch just like Dick Tracy did back in the days when that was only a figment of a comic book artist's imagination.

There are now "invisible fences" that can be installed around a piece of property that will sound an alarm if someone wanders beyond a pre-established boundary. This can be very helpful if a family member has dementia and is a wanderer.

Technology is changing the delivery of healthcare in ways we can't begin to imagine. With the advent of electronic medical records, all your providers can be easily connected and see the same information about you. Doctors are already employing robots to do certain surgeries, enabling the procedures to be more precise or go into spaces smaller than they could using the human eye or hand. Hospitals of the future will have doctors caring for patients from faraway locations, monitoring, examining and even doing surgeries from the comfort of their homes. I'm not sure how I feel about that.

> **Skyping Grandma is no substitute for a hug.**

Some of these devices let us "age at home" and keep us out of nursing homes longer, and that's certainly a good thing.

What's not so good is that the technology of this brave new world is exploding right at the time when Baby Boomers and their parents are least able to adapt to it. Some of these devices are like jigsaw puzzles on steroids. I gave my grandson an electronic superhero last Hanukkah. I opened up the box with all its parts and closed it back up, hyperventilating. My grandson, who was eight at the time, put it together in five minutes.

We're not completely lost in cyberspace, however. Fifty-three percent of people over age 65 use the internet, and 70 percent of those use it daily. The three most common electronic devices used by seniors are the cellphone, computer and music player (iPod or mp3 player).

Despite all the advances in technology there are still plenty of "old-fangled" ways you can make your life better or safer that don't come with an instruction manual the size of the Manhattan phone book.

Take the rubber bathmat, for example. Get rid of mats that have suction cups, because the foot can get caught and you'll fall through the shower door. You can replace it with no slip strips for pennies.

Turn the water heater down to 120 degrees to eliminate any chance of burns.

Retrofit the bathroom with a bathtub or shower that doesn't require stepping into.

All-in-all I think technology is a good news story, but not when it comes at the expense of losing the personal touch. My concern is that people have started substituting human touch and physical interaction with the electronic kind—even when they don't have to. It concerns me that family members who live close by are finding it easier to connect electronically. Skyping Grandma is no substitute for stopping by to give her a hug.

Technology has seemingly made us feel more connected (all those people wouldn't be emailing you stupid jokes if they didn't think they were your friends, would they?). In reality I believe we are actually less connected, because we are interacting in person less. We feel plugged in to the outside world, but it's artificial. It's a golden handcuff.

Enjoy the banquet of marvelous technology that calls to you, but don't allow it to delude you into thinking that's all you or your loved one needs.

And buyer beware. Just because there's a device that does something unique doesn't mean you need it.

Electric fork, anyone? No thanks. Just pass the potatoes.

Chapter Twelve

Going Out with a Bang: Sex After 60

I walked into a certain senior center one morning, which I won't name, to encounter the women at the reception desk giggling and snickering like schoolgirls. Of course I was curious about what was so darn funny, so I asked.

It seems that the night before, a group of "mature" singles (60+) had held their monthly get together (with about six women for every man, of course). As one car after the next exited the parking lot, the security guard prepared to lock up the gate. But there was one problem. Two cars remained, with no one in sight. After waiting a few minutes for someone to come out of the building, the guard noticed a man sitting behind the wheel of one of the cars. As the guard approached, the man frantically waved him off, signaling to "wait a minute." About five minutes later, the guard saw a woman's head pop up in the passenger side. She then exited the car, got into her own, and they both drove off. It didn't take much deduction to figure out what had happened, and the guard ended up with a good story about that night, but his story wasn't as good as the one the unnamed man had to tell who was sitting in that particular driver's seat.

Sex, it turns out, is still an important part of life for both men and women well into their later years.

I still chuckle when I think about this story a friend of mine told with one of those "Oh, God, I just bit into a lemon" kind of faces.

One day he went to visit his parents, 85 and 83, who were living in an assisted living community. He knocked on the door several times, but no one answered. Worried, he went down to the office to get a key. He let himself in and heard noises in the bedroom. He looked in and saw his parents naked, red-faced and hysterically laughing. Were they doing it like they had when they were young? Probably not, but that's OK. They were still doing it!

Sex after 60 isn't likely to be the way it was in the good ol' days. Just ask Toby Keith, whose lyrics sum it up for us Baby Boomers: "I ain't as good as I once was but I'm as good once as I ever was."

Without a doubt sex at this age presents its own unique challenges and circumstances. Men have problems with erections, ejaculation and desire. Women can experience vaginal dryness, lowered libido and embarrassment about how they look.

Medical science can help address the medical challenges, and a little knowledge about male psychology can give you ladies a reason to relax if you're worried about your body, so listen up: men don't care if your arms or breasts sag a little or you're not shaped the way you once were. They're not looking at that. They're just happy they're getting lucky. Yes, even at this age.

Thanks to ED drugs (a $5 billion a year business), people over 60 are having more sex than their parents did. And while I'm not going to talk about my sex life I can tell you this: If I had an erection for more than four hours I wouldn't call my doctor, I'd call a hooker!

"I'm as good once as I ever was."

Many older people report that sex is better than it was when they were young. It usually takes more time, and this increases intimacy. It's not just about hanging onto your youth (though for some much older ladies it might be about attracting a man who drives at night). No matter how old you are, you need love and affection, and sex is a powerful (and pleasurable) way to get it.

I've had some fun with this chapter but now I'm going to get serious. Unlike the unfettered and free 60s (1960s, that is), irresponsible sex can be dangerous.

Although sex at this age carries no worries about pregnancy, health risks are very real, exactly the same risks people half your age face.

Case in point: The Villages in Florida, the largest gated over-55 community in the world.

In 2009 the New York Post labeled it "ground zero for geriatrics who are seriously getting it on." It described residents having sex in the ubiquitous golf carts and a seedy Viagra black market rivaling some back alleys outside their stately walls. One police officer told the newspaper: "You see two 70-year-olds with canes fighting over a woman and you think, 'Oh, jeez.'" So, you ask, What's the problem?

Sexually transmitted diseases.

That's the problem.

STD's have run rampant there.

According to the Post article, between 1995 and 2005 STD rates spiraled upward at a breathtaking rate: reported cases of gonorrhea went from 152 to 245; syphilis cases doubled from 17 to 33; and chlamydia jumped from 52 to 115 cases. A local gynecologist told the Post reporter that she treated more cases of herpes and human papillomavirus at The Villages than she had when she worked in Miami.

No matter how old you are, you need love and affection.

As of this year, nearly 50 percent of all new diagnosed cases of HIV in the United States are predicted to be seniors. People don't realize that 60-year-old men are dating 35-year-old women and, like the educators say, they are sleeping with everyone else that their partner slept with.

That being said, the best thing you can do if you find yourself widowed or divorced and out in the world for the first time in years is to educate yourself about disease prevention. Just like "back in the day" at the local make-out place, a lowly condom could once again be your best friend.

Enjoy!

Chapter Thirteen

Please Just Make Sure I'm Dead

Years ago there was a delightful TV show hosted by Art Linkletter called *Kids Say the Darndest Things*. You just never knew what bit of wit or wisdom would come out of the mouths of those babes. Well, not long ago I found myself in what I think could have been called Caregivers Say the Darndest Things after a meeting I attended left me wide-eyed and thinking about something I had never thought much about before.

As owner of a home healthcare company I make it a point to be visible in the community among groups who might benefit from what I do. One of those groups is a support group for caregivers of people who have Alzheimer's disease or are survivors of people who had it.

The upbeat topic of this one particular caregiver support group was funeral arrangements. No one was knocking down the door for that one, but there were eight brave souls who showed up to talk and to learn about what nobody really wants to talk or to learn about.

As we went around the table, each person was asked what they wanted to happen to them when they died. This is what I heard:

- Donate my body to science

- Be cremated and separate my ashes into two urns for my two children

- Donate my organs

- Put me in a mausoleum

- Bury me in the ground

- Scatter my ashes from a helicopter

- Bury me alongside my first husband, not my second!

- Send my body up North to the family plot

To my amazement every single one of those eight people had said something different. Who knew there were so many choices? I sure as heck didn't. I suddenly realized that death isn't all that simple. In fact, it's more complicated than that other inevitability we call taxes.

After I left that day I set out on a mission to find out more and quickly learned that what I had heard at that support group was only a small sampling of possibilities.

I had thought about death, of course. My own father had died a few years ago, but I hadn't really pondered how many options there were for arrangements and how treacherous the landscape is for family members when no one plans ahead.

I reflected back on my father's funeral and realized that I had spent way too much money on it because (1) he had never expressed his wishes and (2) I was emotionally off balance and not in a good frame of mind to make a sound financial decision.

Here's my personal cautionary tale.

My father had been living in Las Vegas when he died. He had never discussed anything with anybody about his final wishes–at least as far as my sisters and stepmother knew. I flew there from New York, walked into the funeral home and was horrified by

> **"Bury me next to my first husband, not my second."**

what I saw: My father was "resting" in a plain pine box. Now, this happens to be Jewish custom, so I shouldn't have been all that shocked, but I was. After all, he was my father, and I was in a position to see that his send-off was far fancier than that. So, guess what I did?

I forked over $5,000 for an extravagant casket for him. Well, in hindsight it wasn't really for him.

It was more for me. I wanted to feel better about it, to do one last generous act for him. I wasn't thinking clearly. It might not even have been what my father would have wanted.

When there are no plans in place, families really don't have a sense of what their loved one wanted. When you make decisions at the time of need, you will almost always overspend.

> **It might not even have been what my father would have wanted.**

Also, when siblings don't know their parents' wishes this can cause conflict. "Dad would not have wanted it that way," one will say, while the other insists, "That's exactly what Dad would have wanted." It can get even more complicated when there are half brothers and sisters and stepparents involved.

Death should be a time to grieve and remember, not to make complicated decisions. You leave a mess behind if there are no instructions about what you want done.

In most cases, this is simply inexcusable. Only about 10 percent of deaths are sudden and unexpected. That means 90 percent of us will have the time and opportunity to do this one tremendous act of love for our families.

Because there are so many questions that come up these days, the best thing your parents can do for you, and the best thing you can do for your children, is to get this out in the open, make the hard decisions, let everybody know about them, and go on with your life.

Virtually every issue within a family pertaining to a death occurs because nobody planned for it.

Get a grip on the financial, emotional and familial implications of your death to avoid family squabbles, confusion, misunderstanding and unnecessary expense.

Here are some examples of the types of questions that should be answered by you for your children and by your parents for you:

Do you want to be buried or cremated?

If you want to be cremated, what should be done with your ashes? Who should get them? Should they be kept or spread? If spread, where, how and when?

If you want to be buried, should it be under a shady tree, next to Grandma or above ground in a mausoleum?

If you choose a mausoleum, which one? On which floor?

Is there already a purchased plot? If so, where is it? If not, where would you like to be buried? This is particularly important to establish for people who have homes in two different states.

If you've bought a cemetery plot or pre-need contract and you move, how does that affect your benefits? Can you get a refund? If so, how and how much?

Death should be a time to grieve, not make complicated decisions.

Do you want to be buried alongside your spouse? If so, should it be side-by-side or head-to-toe?

What if you want to be buried and your wife wants to be cremated? Does she want her ashes with you in your casket or somewhere else?

What if you and your spouse are from different religions? For example, if you want to be buried in a Jewish cemetery, can your non-Jewish wife be buried there, too?

If you were married before, do you want to be buried with your previous or your most recent spouse?

If you're a veteran, do you want to be buried in a veteran's cemetery? Which one? Is that OK with your spouse?

Do you want your arrangements to follow your religious background to the letter or is there room for deviation? For example, cremation has been a big no-no among Jews for centuries, but many Jews these days are choosing it as a more economical option.

Who do you want in charge of your final arrangements? You should designate someone, along with an alternate.

Do you want a headstone? If so, what kind? What size? What do you want it to say? (I joke with my golfing buddies that my headstone should say, "This is Scott's first hole-in-one," since I've never had one—at least not yet.)

Do you want a funeral or a memorial service or nothing at all? If you want a service, where should it be?

You get the point....for something so complex it amazes me that most of us are pretty much clueless.

Now, as long as we're on this very maudlin subject, I want to give you another list. This one involves documents that will be needed after you die (or in at least one case, beforehand). Please note that I am not an attorney and this is not intended as a complete list, but it represents many of the most commonly-needed documents. Consult an attorney to determine all of the documents that your particular situation calls for.

You not only need to have these documents, but you also must, and I repeat must, let key family members know that you have them and where they are. You can give them to your attorney or have them in a secure place at home that trusted family members know how to access. The kindest thing you can do is have every pertinent document in one place so that it's not a hardship on your family to try to collect them:

Original copy of your will.

Ownership documents of all valuable assets such as real estate, cars, cemetery plots, investments and business partnerships.

A list of all your bank accounts with online login information.

Tax returns from the last three years (obviously you will need to update these over the years).

Copies of all life insurance policies. While an insurance company is bound to pay agreed-upon death benefits when a claim is submitted, they are not required to keep track of whether you are still alive. If your family doesn't know about these policies, they won't be able to collect on them.

Copies of all accounts containing pensions, IRA's, stocks and bonds .

Location of all safety deposit boxes, along with the keys. Make sure one of your family members is on the registration document so they can access the boxes.

Healthcare power of attorney, so healthcare decisions can

be made if you are unable to do so.

Marriage certificate, so your spouse can prove that you and he/she were married.

Copy of child support orders.

NOTE: *Think carefully about any documents you might be considering keeping in a safe deposit box, as most boxes cannot be accessed 24/7.*

The takeaway of this chapter is that it's really important to let your family know what your plans are, make those plans in advance, understand what you are buying, insure that your wishes are honored and to give your family the gift of allowing them to grieve.

Oh, and one more thing. You can learn a lot about pre-need planning on the internet. One good website is http://www.dignitymemorial.com/.

Now, go out and eat a good meal.

Tell someone special you love them and enjoy the rest of your life.

Chapter Fourteen

You're Never Too Old to Have a Purpose

"The purpose of life is not to be happy. It is to be useful, to be honorable, to be compassionate, to have it make some difference that you have lived and lived well."

Ralph Waldo Emerson

In 2007 I went to the funeral in New York of a dear friend who had died at 62 of pancreatic cancer. She was a wonderful wife and mother, a successful Realtor in New York and Florida, and was a champion amateur golfer. The room was packed. People had flown in from all over the country. I said to my friend sitting next to me, damn, would you look at this crowd! I knew she was well-known, but this was over the top. My friend replied to me: When you're the first to go, everybody shows up. When you're the last, your service is at the graveside, and they just roll you in.

It was kind of funny, but it also rang true, and it got me thinking about people who have reached the age where many of their friends are gone, often their spouses are gone, and their lives look absolutely nothing like they did five or ten years earlier.

Finding a purpose: a reason to get up in the morning.

I see it in my business all the time—clients who've become progressively more isolated and, as a result, are depressed, feeling hopeless and just waiting for their turn to get rolled into the grave. They've stopped playing cards three times a week. They no longer go out to dinner with friends, and the widow's club they were active in has shrunk from eight to three, one with dementia and the other two unable to drive. Before you know it they are spending more and more time alone in front of the TV doing crossword puzzles and never leaving the house.

Nobody depends on them, and they don't depend on anyone.

How many times have you heard stories about people who were dead for days because there was no one checking on them, and no one knew anything was wrong?

It really bothers me when I hear about people in any of those circumstances because I know that in almost every situation, incorporating one small change can make all the difference in how they feel about their lives and the time they have left.

That small change is finding a purpose: a reason to get up in the morning.

Finding a purpose can happen at any age, and it can take different forms throughout our lives. Raising your children might have been a purpose 40 years ago. Taking care of an ill parent might have been another a few years later. Working side-by-side with your spouse to build a future for your family could have filled that place. And now? You are left thinking you're too old and there's no way you can contribute to the world.

Stop! Do not pass Go! Do not collect $200!

You can sit back and bemoan your situation (Waah! Waah! Nothing is like it used to be) and get progressively more depressed, passive and resentful like the woman in this Yiddish joke whose son finally calls. Here's their conversation:

> Son: Mom, you don't sound so good.
> Mom: I haven't eaten in four days.
> Son: Why?
> Mom: I didn't want to be in the kitchen in case you should call.

Your other choice? Take control, get off your behind and find something to do where your talents, skills and wisdom can be applied and appreciated. Once I retire, I want to stay so busy with life passions that my children need a GPS device to keep track of me.

One of the best ways you can find a purpose is to volunteer (this is a far different experience than writing a check, which you should also consider doing, if you can afford to).

It doesn't matter if you can't drive or you have physical impairments or your typing is rusty or your wardrobe isn't fashionable. There will be something you can contribute to society, and trust me when I tell you, you will get far more out of it than the people will whom you helped.

Let me tell you a story about myself. I grew up very poor in a low income neighborhood in Queens, New York and was an underperforming student in school. Because of my lousy grades and no family connections to grease the skids, there wasn't a single college I applied to that would accept me. Even open enrollment schools rejected my applications. To give myself something to do while I figured out my path in life, I began volunteering with an organization that helped developmentally challenged children. I loved it, and the man who ran the organization was so impressed with me that he wrote a recommendation letter for me which resulted in my finally being accepted into college.

> **You simply never know where volunteering will lead.**

Another big plus, one I could never have imagined, was that a pretty young woman named Irene was also volunteering for that organization, and that's how I met my wife of 43 years!

The point of this is that you simply never know where volunteering will lead. There is something magical about giving back and volunteering, and that magic has the potential to change a life (yours as well as others').

I knew a man whose son died tragically in his 30s. The father went into a deep depression and stayed there for years. Nothing seemed to help. Eventually he began mentoring a young boy, and slowly his depression subsided. That boy, now a young man, loves to tell how my friend changed his life. My friend always responds, "Yes, but you changed my life even more."

Volunteering is good for your mind and body. People who volunteer tend to be healthier and happier because they have a purpose. Volunteering forces you to get up and take a shower and put on clean clothes and get out of the house. If you're having a bad day, you still have a reason to get up. You meet new people, make new friends and now have folks in your life who would check on you if you didn't show up when you were supposed to.

Engaging yourself in something meaningful and challenging helps keep your mind young. Socializing reduces isolation.

Ask yourself what kinds of causes and issues interest you. Disadvantaged or sick children? Handicapped people? Animals? Diseases like breast cancer? Battered women? Education?

The list is endless.

Now here's the tough love: No one is going to beat down your door to volunteer. You have to be proactive by picking up the phone and making some calls or contacting friends and family to find out what they are doing that you might enjoy. The following list below is there just to give you an idea of where to start. You can get more ideas, and more information about volunteering at www.worldvolunteerweb.com.

> Churches
> Synagogues
> United Way
> Senior centers
> Public and private schools
> Food banks
> Soup kitchens
> Veterans' organizations
> Mentoring programs like Foster Grandparents and Big Brothers/Big Sisters

Volunteering impacts the community, gives you motivation for life, offers the opportunity for you to achieve something, allows you to utilize your abilities and talents, and introduces you to new people. Once you start, there will always be someone whose eyes light up when you walk into a room. It's unbelievably powerful...I think you get the picture.

It's never too late to experience those benefits. It's in everyone's best interest when a senior shows up and does something good for someone else (if you're housebound, there are organizations you can do phone work for, or lick envelopes).

The only thing that is holding you back from changing your life for the better is you. I've volunteered all my life, and I've never regretted one day of it. Do something about it today. The quality of your life and your mental health depend on it.

Afterword

The process of writing this book has been an adventure to say the least. I couldn't have accomplished this without the help of many people, most notably my writing partner Gwen Carden and, of course, my daughter and business partner Allison Negri. My wife Irene, who I mention often throughout these pages, also contributed her advice and counsel regularly, and most of the time it was very much appreciated.

Narrowing down topics to cover was difficult. There is so much to talk about regarding the journey that is the aging dynamic. I am concerned that I have left out some very important information gleaned from over 100 radio shows and countless meetings with families and clients over the years. Unfortunately, I couldn't fit it all into one coherent tome without this book being a whole lot bigger than it is, which is why I've already begun to formulate my next book to include the topics I left out due to space constraints.

One of the subjects I haven't addressed in this book, but one that is truly critical, is the tragic epidemic of Alzheimer's disease and dementia in this country. This oncoming tsunami will potentially affect an unbelievable number of families in the years to come. In fact, by some statistics nearly one in two people who reach age 85 will experience some level of dementia. Given that that demographic is the largest growing population in the United States by percentage, if that doesn't scare you nothing will.

If we don't find a cure soon, the resulting costs associated with this disease will overwhelm us. This is not to mention the emotional impact that comes with the financial costs as families confront the reality of a disease that can go on for ten years or more. When you add in the chronic diseases of Parkinson's, MS, ALS and others, we really need to focus on the things we must do to be prepared for what lies ahead. So while I've tried to put an upbeat and sometimes humorous spin on the topics covered in this book, trust me, getting older is really serious business.

I hope I've opened some eyes and helped people look at what they have to do before they face a crisis, because it probably won't be too long before your children will be saying about you, "Oh, my God, I'm getting older and so is my mom."

About The Author

Scott Greenberg is host of the weekly radio show "Oh My God, I'm Getting Older and So Is My Mom" on Seaview Radio in Palm Beach, Florida. He also serves as President of Palm Beach ComForcare Senior Services, a private duty non-medical home healthcare agency serving all of Palm Beach, Martin, St. Lucie and Indian River Counties in South Florida.

Scott is active in local healthcare initiatives and activities as a result of his business and his radio show. He currently serves as President of the Florida State Guardianship Association and is Treasurer of the Palm Beach County Partnership for Aging. In addition to those duties, he is also an elected member of the Advisory Council of the Area Agency on Aging and has served on the Alzheimer's Community Care Goodwill Task Force.

Prior to purchasing controlling interest in Palm Beach ComForcare, Scott was President of Curran and Connors, Inc., the nation's largest designer of corporate annual reports. He grew C&C from a small, one studio design firm into 16 offices including four design studios across the United States. During his tenure, the firm was twice named one of Long Island's 25 fastest growing companies by KPMG, one of the largest professional services companies in the world, and Small Business of the Year by the Hauppauge Industrial Association. Scott was also nominated as a finalist in Ernst & Young's Entrepreneur of the Year program and was one of only six businessmen in the New York metropolitan area selected to judge Arthur Andersen's Best Practices Competition for three consecutive years.

Scott has been called on regularly to speak on topics of importance to various audiences. A full list of his speaking venues and topics can be seen on the Speaking Engagements tab of his website www.omgimgettingolderandsoismymom.com.

Scott resides in Boca Raton, Florida with wife, Irene, of 43 years.

You can always contact Scott directly, and he welcomes your outreach. He is also available to speak to your group.

Below is his contact information:

Snail mail
Scott Greenberg
333, LLC
9121 N. Military Trail, Suite 216
Palm Beach Gardens, FL 33410

E-mail
slg123@comcast.net

Phone
(561) 706-5157

Endorsements

"This book is a must read for everyone concerned about a loved one's later years as well as their own. Scott is a leader in providing practical, no-nonsense and entertaining information on aging issues. His experience and sense of humor presents practical information in an entertaining read."

Michelle Hollister
Elder Law Attorney and
President of the National Guardianship Association

"As Clerk, we see those who must use the court system to manage their lives through our criminal, guardianship, and probate divisions. Through Scott's experience and sense of humor, we can begin a thoughtful, proactive preparation for aging gracefully with dignity. All mature readers and caregivers will gain knowledge and a perspective suitable for sharing and empowering."

Sharon R. Bock, Esq.
Clerk & Comptroller, Palm Beach County

"Scott dedicates himself to being a vehicle for delivering valuable and useful information to elders looking to increase their knowledge and improve their quality of life. I enjoy working with Scott because of his passion for senior issues and his commitment to improving the lives of the elder population. I am proud to call him a friend."

State Representative Mark S. Pafford
District 86

"Having had the pleasure of knowing Scott personally and professionally, I feel I must weigh in. In the world of aging, I come across all kinds of people who work in this field, but there are two kinds that stand out in my mind: those who mainly work for the paycheck, and those who care more about the seniors they serve. Scott exemplifies the latter in more ways than one. He knows how difficult it is for families emotionally and financially when it comes to finding help for their aging loved ones. He knows how confusing it can be for the families to negotiate their way around the ins and outs of this fast growing field. If you're looking for Scott's heart, you'll find it in his work...and it shows in the hours he invests–as he's always available when you need him. You see, of the two types of workers I mentioned, no matter how committed and hard-working these caregivers are, there can be an ocean of difference in how they give care. Scott Greenberg is the very definition of "caring".... especially when it comes to seniors."

Jaime Estremera-Fitzgerald
Chief Executive Officer, Area Agency on Aging
Your Aging Resource Center

"Scott is "a real gift" to seniors in our community. He has also shown a serious commitment to the industry that serves this targeted demographic. Scott educates seniors about their options, their rights, and helps them identify their needs by priority. South Florida has become the capital for this age group and Scott has emerged as one of the clear-cut leaders in educating seniors and bringing the industry who serve them together to help make the services easier to navigate."

Bruce H. Berns
Publisher of Nostalgic America Magazine

"There are not many people who you can say are your mentors but to me, Scott is one of my mentors. He is an ethical, moral, hardworking, dedicated husband, father, and friend. It is my pleasure to do business with Scott as well as call him my friend."

> Karen Greene
> *CEO Hired Hearts and President of the South Florida*
> *Guardianship Association, Palm Beach Chapter*

"Without reading the future book, I already know it will be filled with a view point that depicts how much you care for others. You are a natural caregiver and want so much for those who are vulnerable and fragile to be protected and valued. Those are virtues that others should emulate."

> Mary Barnes
> *President and CEO*
> *Alzheimer's Community Care*

"Scott has been an inspiration for me personally as well as the audience of Seaview Radio. His uncompromising commitment to finding the best for seniors has brought an unparalleled level of respect to the senior care arena. He is a leader in this field. It is said that leadership is nothing but influence. Scott has the influence. Everywhere I go people comment about the content on his show and how ethical he is. Scott's leadership has impacted all who have come in contact with him. Leaders like Scott have touched the heart of many seniors before he asked for their hand. Scott has been as asset to the community and to the growth of our radio station. I am proud to know Scott and call him a friend."

> Chet Tart
> *Vice President & General Manager*
> *Seaview Radio*

"Scott continues to apply passion and great energy to help improve the future for aging baby-boomers and elderly throughout his community. His laser like focus and no-nonsense approach is truly remarkable and an inspiration for others to model."

Mark Armstrong
President & CEO
ComForcare Senior Services

"Scott has an innate ability to connect with all types of people. He maintains a youthfully inquisitive nature in regards to other peoples well-being. These are rare and indispensable qualities, extremely beneficial in the works that he does for others."

Richard A. Levine
MD FACP, Board Certified in Internal Medicine
Priority Concierge MD

"As you know, I have just finished being a caregiver for the last three years for my ailing wife. Having run a few large businesses I thought I was well equipped to navigate the issues and decisions that presented themselves. I only wish I had read this book and the advice you offer as it would have made the journey much easier for both of us."

Denis Connors
Founder, Curran & Connors, Inc. and Lifelong Friend

"As a physician, knowing that Scott Greenberg and his team are out there helping to care for our most frail, elderly patients gives me great comfort. Scott is a successful entrepreneur with a kind-hearted soul. In a word, Scott is a mensch!"

Stuart J. Bagatell, MD
Board Certified in Internal Medicine

"Scott has enacted a stage of life transformation many have contemplated but few do. Following a successful career, he "retired" and did the whole "around the world" later life crisis thing. He returned home to discover that retirement wasn't what we imagined it to be and it was time for a "third age" reality check. Focusing on the inevitability of aging, he carved out a business opportunity in home healthcare, but soon recognized that its image, expectations and protocols for an aging America left a lot to be desired. His insights and pragmatism have created a book that teaches and educates but also lays out a practical perspective and planning approach to America's greatest enigma–aging and dementia. This book is a must read if only to appreciate the perspective of a true hands on, entrepreneurial businessman with a heart and a passion for what he is doing and the industry changes he is driving."

David J Levy JD, CCE
Gerontologist
Eldercare Mediator, Family Caregiver Expert,
Family Caregiver Advocacy Group

Share
OMG, I'm Getting Older and So Is My Mom
With Others

To order individual copies (less than 100) of the book:
Call 561-630-1620 M-F 9am-5pm EST

Also available at:
Local bookstores
Amazon.com
www.omgimgettingolderandsoismymom.com

OMG, I'm Getting Older and So Is My Mom
ISBN 978-1-884886-64-5

$15 ea + $6.75 shipping & handling (1-3 copies)